Amstrad Word Processing

on the PCW 8256

Ian Sinclair

COLLINS
8 Grafton Street, London W1

Collins Professional and Technical Books
William Collins Sons & Co. Ltd
8 Grafton Street, London W1X 3LA

First published in Great Britain by
Collins Professional and Technical Books 1986
Reprinted 1986

British Library Cataloguing in Publication Data
Sinclair, Ian R.
Amstrad word processing: on the PCW 8256.
1. Word processing   2. Amstrad Microcomputer
I. Title
652′.5′02854165   Z.52.5A4/

ISBN 0–00–383328–3

Typeset by V & M Graphics Ltd, Aylesbury, Bucks
Printed and bound in Great Britain by
Mackays of Chatham, Kent

Other books of interest

Introducing Amstrad CP/M Assembly Language
Ian Sinclair
0 00 383309 7

Advanced Amstrad CPC6128 Computing
Ian Sinclair
0 00 383300 3

The Automated Office
Joseph St. John Bate and Ross Burgess
0 00 383008 X

Contents

Preface

The Amstrad PCW 8256 is the computer which has made possible word processing for all. It is suited to the small office, the small section of a large office, the home user – anyone who needs to put words on paper. Many buyers of this excellent machine, however, will have been overwhelmed by the sheer volume of reading material in the manuals, and may have found it difficult to know where to start in word processing. This book is a step-by-step guide to word processing with the PCW 8256. It makes very little mention of the computing uses of the machine using CP/M, BASIC or LOGO, because these other facilities are of little interest to you when you need the machine purely for word processing. If, however, you intend to use the PCW 8256 also for other business purposes, such as running spreadsheets, databases or 'thought-organisers', then you will need to consult other books on the use of the CP/M operating system such as mine, published by Collins, entitled *Introducing Amstrad CP/M Assembly Language*. If you intend to write programs for yourself in the BASIC language, you will need a book devoted to the 'Mallard BASIC', which is *not* completely identical to the BASIC that is used in other Amstrad machines. It's most unlikely that you will want to use the LOGO language for any kind of business application.

This book, then, is devoted to word processing. A few years ago, the facilities provided by the PCW 8256 would have cost several thousands of pounds, and might not have been accompanied by the computing power which is also available to you with this machine. As a result, the PCW 8256 is generally bought by users who might never have used a word processor, and may not even have used an electric typewriter. Because of this, every effort has been made in this book to cater for the complete beginner to word processing, bearing in mind that you, the reader, probably have very little time for reading about the machine. To that end, this book is organised with the aim of being compact, leaving the manual as the ultimate reference book. Where there would be no point in repeating a set of instructions, reference has been made to the manual, but the aim has been to make this book as self-sufficient as possible, so that you have only one book to cope with at a time. Above all, the aim is to get as much useful experience as possible, because practice makes perfect in word processing as in every other craft.

I am most grateful to Mark Newton and Rhett Houghton of Sudbury Microsystems, who supplied me with a PCW 8256 at very short notice. I must also pay tribute to Richard Miles of Collins Professional and Technical Books, who commissioned this book, and to Janet Murphy and Sue Moore, also at Collins, who made sense of it all.

Ian Sinclair

Section One
Setting Up

Note

Where [+] appears in the text it means the ⊞ key.
Where [–] appears in the text it means the ⊟ key.

You should connect the units of the system together, as guided by the manual. There is not a great length of connecting cable between the units, and you will need to place the keyboard, monitor and printer fairly close to each other. This is made much easier if you can use a computing desk, such as the type illustrated in Figure 1.1. Either the monitor or the printer can be placed on the higher shelf, and the low shelf can be used for paper, discs and other accessories. If you are working on a plain desk, it's easier to place the monitor behind the keyboard, and put the printer to one side. Make sure that the connectors are firmly in place, but do not attempt to force them. The large printer plug will fit only one way round in its socket, and this is also true of the plug on the end of the cable from the keyboard, which fits only one way round in the socket at the side of the monitor. The connection point that is marked 'EXPANSION' is for use with an additional disc drive, and you can ignore it if you have no second drive.

The keyboard of the PCW 8256 is set out very like the keyboard of an electric typewriter, but with a lot of extra keys. All the ordinary letter and number keys behave very much as they do on an electric typewriter, with the difference that almost all of them will repeat their action when held down. You must get into the habit of striking a key firmly and releasing it right away, rather than holding the key down while you think about the next one. Unlike a typewriter, the key action is silent. There is only a slight click when you press a key, and this can be disconcerting to an experienced typist. In addition, the keys which are used to control the action of the machine behave very differently from keys on a typewriter. One annoying difference is that the SHIFT LOCK action applies to the top row of (number) keys as well as to the letter keys.

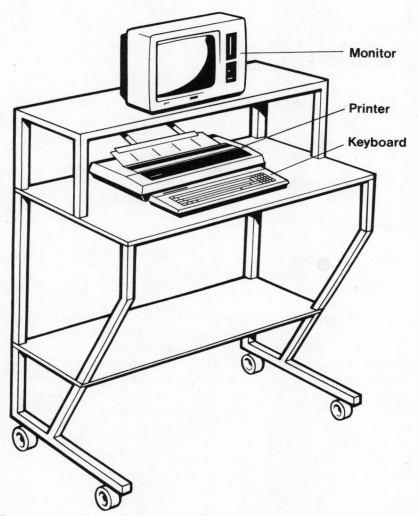

Monitor

Printer

Keyboard

Figure 1.1. A computing desk, such as the type made by Selmor, is ideal for housing the PCW 8256 components.

We'll look at the actions of a lot of the special keys as we come to them, but one in particular, the RETURN key, must be understood right away. This key is located where an electric typewriter has its CARRIAGE RETURN key, but the RETURN key of the PCW 8256 is used in a very different way, both in word processing and (particularly) when the machine is being used as a computer. In this latter case, the RETURN key is used to make the machine obey a typed command or instruction. There is also a key marked ENTER which is used for word processing, but which should be avoided when you are using the machine as a computer. In earlier Amstrad models, the ENTER and RETURN key names were used almost interchangeably, so this can be confusing. We'll see how the RETURN and ENTER keys are used in word processing later, but for the moment we'll remind you when such a key needs to be pressed by putting (press RETURN), (press ENTER) or just (RETURN) or (ENTER).

Once you have fitted all the pieces together, you have an empty computer. I use the word empty because until you put a program into it, a computer is as useless as a record-player with no records. The programs for the computer are contained on the two discs that are provided in the package. Several of these programs are very precious, and unless you have bought several PCW 8256s, your first action must be to make copies of the discs. The most important disc to copy is the one which is marked LOCO SCRIPT on one side, and CP/M PLUS on the other. If anything happens to erase the programs on this disc, particularly on the LOCO SCRIPT side, you will find

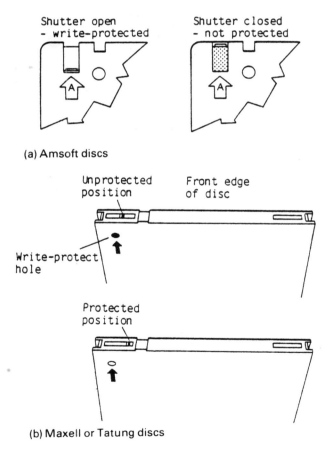

Figure 1.2. The write-protect systems found on the two disc types that can be obtained.

it expensive to replace. Of the two sides, the one that you particularly need to copy is the LOCO SCRIPT side. In my PCW 8256, a large reminder sheet, printed in red, was tucked in under the packing. The most important point to understand at this stage is that you must always *remove any disc from the drive before switching on or off*. The act of switching on or off can generate enough magnetism near the disc to alter some stored codes. This can make the disc 'corrupted' and therefore unusable. This is one of the main reasons for needing to take a copy of very important discs.

Copying LOCO SCRIPT

You *must* make a copy of LOCO SCRIPT, because the program as supplied is not suitable for everyday use. To use LOCO SCRIPT, you need to be able to put (write) information on to the disc as well as read it off the disc. The 'master' discs that are supplied with the machine can be read only, not written. The only way that these master discs can be written is by covering the write-protect holes (see Figure 1.2) with opaque Sellotape, and if you have only one copy of each master disc, you should not attempt to do this. Figure 1.3, then, shows the steps in making a copy of the LOCO SCRIPT disc side.

1. Remove disc, switch off completely.
2. Switch on machine and insert CP/M disc, with title **CP/M PLUS** facing left.
3. Wait until the screen displays **A>**.
4. Type DISCKIT (or disckit), press the RETURN or ENTER key.
5. When screen menu appears, remove disc and turn it so that the LOCO SCRIPT side faces left. Insert the disc this way round.
6. Press **f5** key. Screen message asks for confirmation. Press **Y** key to confirm, then wait for next message.
7. Message on screen is 'Insert disc to write'. Put in new disc and press RETURN, ENTER or SPACEBAR. Wait.
8. Message on screen is 'Insert disc to read'. Replace LOCO SCRIPT disc, title to left again. Press RETURN, ENTER or SPACEBAR. Wait.
9. Message on screen is 'Insert disc to write'. Remove LOCO SCRIPT disc, replace new disc. Press RETURN, ENTER or SPACEBAR. Wait.
10. Message is 'Remove disc'. Do this, then press any key other than **Y** to stop copying the program.
11. Press EXIT when final menu appears. The **A>** will reappear on the top left-hand side of the screen.
12. With no disc in place, press keys EXTRA, SHIFT and EXIT together. Insert your new LOCO SCRIPT copy. Machine is now ready for word processing with the copy of LOCO SCRIPT. This is your Start-of-day disc.

Figure 1.3. Copying the LOCO SCRIPT disc so that the copy can be used as your Start-of-day disc. This disc will be used when the computer is switched on, but you will probably want to replace it with a data disc thereafter

Once you have made a copy of LOCO SCRIPT on one side of a disc, you can put the original master disc away in a safe place. Your copy is the one that will be used from now on. It is your disc for word processing, and is referred to in the manual and in this book as the 'Start-of-day' disc, a title that is best not abbreviated.

Figure 1.4 shows the precautions you should take with discs to prevent damage. The most serious damage is caused by invisible magnetism, so discs must never be kept on top of the monitor, or near any device (other than the disc drive itself) which contains an electric motor.

When you have made a copy of LOCO SCRIPT, you can check it by typing DIR (or dir) and then pressing RETURN. This display does not show all of the programs that are on the master disc. A full list, obtained from a printout,

---

Care of discs

1. Keep discs in their protective boxes when they are not inserted in the drive. If you drop a box, it will chip, but this is better than chipping the disc jacket.
2. Buy discs from a reputable source, such as Amsoft or one of the large disc suppliers. At these prices, you can't afford to take risks.
3. Never pull back the protective shutter unless you need to – which is normally never!
4. Never touch any part of the inner disc.
5. Keep your discs away from dust, liquids, smoke, heat and sunlight.
6. Avoid at all costs magnets and objects that contain magnets. These include electric motors, shavers, TV receivers and monitors, telephones, tape erasers, electric typewriters, and many other items which have surfaces that you might lay discs onto.
7. Label your discs well. If the label on the disc is not large enough, use self-adhesive labels in addition – but don't cover any of the shutters.
8. Remember that the disc is read and written from the *underside*.

Figure 1.4. Some of the precautions for using and storing discs.

is shown in Figure 1.5. The program J11LOCO.EMS is the main word processing program, assisted by JOYCEDIT.JOY. This latter program, incidentally, shows why the machine is often referred to as the 'Joyce'.

Once you have a copy of the LOCO SCRIPT program, you can start it running in two ways. If you have been copying discs, and you are still using the machine as a computer, you will see the sign A $>$ on the screen. Put the LOCO SCRIPT disc into the drive slot, with its title to the left. If you now press the SHIFT, EXTRA and EXIT keys at the same time, LOCO SCRIPT will start running. The alternative is to remove the disc, switch off the machine, then switch on and insert the LOCO SCRIPT disc, title facing left.

```
Directory For Drive B: User  0

  Name    Bytes  Recs  Attributes      Name      Bytes  Recs  Attributes
-------- ------ ----- -----------   ----------- ------ ----- -----------
J11LOCO EMS  43k   344  Sys RW        JOYCEDIT JOY   31k   248  Sys RW
LETTERS GRP   0k     0  Dir RW        MAIL232  COM    4k    32  Sys RW
MATRIX  STD   7k    56  Sys RW        PHRASES  STD    1k     5  Dir RW
READ    ME    6k    42  Dir RW        TEMPLATE STD    1k     4  Dir RW

Total Bytes     =  93k   Total Records  =  731   Files Found =   8
Total 1k Blocks =  93    Used/Max Dir Entries For Drive B:   33/ 64
```

Figure 1.5. The programs that are stored on the LOCO SCRIPT side of the first master disc.

Either way, you will see the bars appear, followed by an announcement, then the Main menu. When you start with word processing on the PCW 8256, these menus are the way you select what you want to do, so we need to look in detail at how to use them.

The Main menu

Use your *copy* of LOCO SCRIPT to load the word processing program. This brings up the Main menu, referred to in the manual as the 'Disc management' menu. The Disc management menu looks rather fearsome at first sight, because there is so much information crammed into it. As in all menus, you normally find that you need only one item and you have to train yourself to find where the item is and concentrate on it. The important portions of the Disc management menu are the green band at the top, and the highlighted parts on the rest of the screen. The green band at the top shows the effects of pressing up to twelve keys, the **C, E, P, D** and **f1** to **f8** keys. The f1 to f8 keys are placed in a vertical column just to the right of the RETURN key. The odd numbers, f1, f3, f5, f7, are obtained by pressing the appropriate key, and the even numbers by pressing one of these keys along with the SHIFT key. On the rest of the menu, the only items of interest at any given time are the pieces that are 'highlighted' by being printed in black on a green background. These indicate what you will be working on.

As the manual describes, you can shift from one item or group to another by using the cursor keys, which are the keys marked with arrows, placed on the right-hand side of the keyboard. You are not limited to the part of the menu that appears on the screen at the time when you start up, as you will see if you hold down the right-arrow key. Since the cursor is the name of the mark that appears on the screen to show you where a typed character will appear, we refer to the highlighting on the menu as a cursor throughout this book. You can move the top cursor (the group cursor) by holding down the SHIFT key as well as pressing the cursor movement key. Using a cursor movement key by itself will move the lower cursor, the document cursor.

The fussy-looking menu starts to make sense when you remove some of the items that are included purely for demonstration purposes. You cannot remove these files, as they are called, from the master disc (unless you cover the write-protect holes), but you can remove them from your copy if you want to. The use of a separate data disc, formatted as described below, makes it unnecessary to delete these files from your Start-of-day disc. If you want to practise erasing files, this is a clumsy and tedious operation, but it is simple. You place the cursor over a filename, press f6 (SHIFT + f5, remember) and look at the little piece of menu that appears to confirm the erasure. You then press ENTER to carry out the 'deletion'. In fact, this does not completely delete the files; it only removes them from the list, and they still take up space. The manual refers to these 'part-deleted' files as being in limbo. To remove the files completely, you have to relist the limbo files, and go through the deleting procedure all over again. Key f8 brings up the Limbo menu, and pressing the [+] key on the left of the spacebar confirms the choice. The limbo files are now displayed, and you can repeat the erasing action on them. You then press ENTER to erase the file. This time, it's gone for keeps! Figure 1.6 gives a summary of this process.

Deleting files

1. Place cursor over filename.
2. Press **f6 (SHIFT f5)**.
3. Message confirms filename.
4. Press ENTER to delete file.
5. Repeat with other files.

This procedure prevents the files from being used in the normal way, and removes them from the listing, but does not erase them completely from the disc. The files are only in 'limbo'. To see the limbo files and delete them completely, carry on as instructed.

6. Press **f8 (SHIFT f7)**.
7. Cursor is on 'Limbo' option. Press [+] key to put in tick, then press ENTER key to confirm this choice. Name of limbo file(s) will be added to listing.
8. Delete limbo file(s) as in steps 1 to 5 above.

Figure 1.6. A summary of the steps in erasing a file.

Making a data disc

The LOCO SCRIPT disc copy, even with the demonstration files removed, leaves too little space for serious work. It should be kept for start-up purposes mainly, and you should record all of your documents on a separate disc. You will need a lot of discs if you are doing anything more than a few letters a day, and you'll find that it pays to buy in bulk. The price of these small discs is very high compared with the $5\frac{1}{2}$ inch size (now around 70p per disc), and you should shop around carefully. The main reason for the high price is that only a few manufacturers make the discs, and only the Amstrad and Tatung machines use them. The blank discs need to be formatted when you want to use them. This means that the disc is magnetically marked out and tested, ready for use. The procedure for formatting is illustrated in Figure 1.7. Once you have a LOCO SCRIPT copy on one disc and a new blank formatted disc ready for text, we can start some word processing.

1. Remove disc, switch off machine completely.
2. Switch machine on and insert CP/M disc, with title **CP/M PLUS** facing left.
3. Wait until the screen displays **A>**.
4. Type DISCKIT (or disckit), press RETURN or ENTER key.
5. When screen menu shows, press **f3** key.
6. Insert disc side to be formatted, facing left. For a new disc, both sides should be formatted.
7. Press **Y** key when disc is in place.
8. The count on top left-hand side of screen goes from 0 to 39 to show the progress of formatting.
9. Screen message asks you to remove disc. At this point, you can press the **Y** key to signal that you want to format the other side.
10. Insert the disc with other side facing left, and press any key to start formatting.
11. When message shows again, press keys as indicated to leave program.
12. With no disc in place, press keys EXTRA, SHIFT and EXIT together. Insert your LOCO SCRIPT copy. Machine is now ready for word processing with the copy of LOCO SCRIPT. The newly formatted disc can be used as a data disc for LOCO SCRIPT use.

Figure 1.7. The procedure for formatting a data disc. Formatting is not needed if you are going to use the disc for a copy of the Start-of-day disc.

Section Two
Direct Printing

Before you can start to get to grips with all the features that a modern word processor can offer, you need to be able to find your way around the ordinary typewriter part of the keyboard. In addition, you need to get accustomed to what the printer of the PCW 8256 can offer. Experience in both can be gained by using what is called direct print mode, in which the whole machine behaves rather like an electronic typewriter. If you haven't been able to get any spare discs, this is about all you can do with it in any case! Joking apart, direct print mode is very useful for brief notes, filling in forms, and in this case, for learning to use the keyboard. Even if you are fairly accustomed to typing, some practice is always needed because no two keyboards ever have all their keys in exactly the same place, particularly keys like the quotes ("), hash (#), and other 'odd' character keys.

To enter direct mode type **D** when the Disc management menu is showing. If any other menu is also showing, press the **CAN**cel key (four keys in from top right) first. If you do not do this, then trying to use a command will cause a beep (a high pitched whistle) of warning from the machine, and the command will not be obeyed. Pressing the **D** key brings up a sub-menu, with the **Confirm** option ticked. To accept this choice, press ENTER. If you want to cancel, move the cursor down one place, and then press ENTER. This will clear the Main menu from your screen, and bring up the direct mode display. If you don't want to go further, you can return by pressing the EXIT key, then confirming by pressing ENTER when the sub-menu appears.

Important note: ENTER is the key that is used to confirm a command to the machine. Pressing ENTER will cause an action to be executed.

To set up in direct mode, *either* (a) load a sheet into the printer (manual, pages 24/25) *or* (b) press the PTR key (second to the right of spacebar). Use the PTR key if you already have a sheet loaded into the printer. This brings up a set of choices at the top of the screen. Assuming that you are using A4 size paper, the only adjustment that you really need to make is setting the left-hand margin for direct typing. This is done by pressing the f3 key to bring up the Actions sub-menu, and then moving the printhead by pressing the cursor movement keys right (and possibly left if you overshoot). This moves the printhead and alters the number that is displayed for offset size on the sub-menu, but does not alter the screen display. Remember the repeating action of these keys! When you have set the left margin, you can return to the Printer menu by pressing ENTER. Pressing ENTER confirms that you have finished setting the printhead position. You can't type while the Printer menu is on the screen, but while it is, its also a good idea to press **f1** for the Options menu, and select Draft quality. The normal setting is High quality, but this is *very* slow. You can select Draft quality, which is certainly good enough for notes, in two ways. The easy way, since the cursor is positioned over the High quality label, is to press the [–] key (right of spacebar), which will shift the tick to the Draft quality label in the sub-menu. The alternative is to move the cursor down to Draft quality and press the [+] key to the left of the spacebar. The action is confirmed as usual by pressing the ENTER key.

Important note: The [+] key can be used to select an option, the [—] key to clear it.

You can now return to the typing page layout by pressing the EXIT key. You will see the screen display and the top band information change to the normal editing layout. The word 'Printing', to the right of top centre, is the only reminder that you are in the direct printing mode.

Simple text

To type text, just type normally as you would with a typewriter *but* with a different use of the RETURN key. As you type, any word that gets to the right-hand margin before its end will *automatically* be put onto the next line. You do *not* need to press RETURN at this point. You don't need to press RETURN unless (a) you want to print just this line of the text, or (b) you need to select a new line following a partial line, perhaps at the end of a paragraph. Always try to keep the use of the RETURN key for selecting a new paragraph, because this is how the key will normally be used in word processing.

To correct the text before printing, use the cursor keys to place the cursor, and the DEL keys (right and left, indicated by arrows) to delete an incorrect character. If you place the cursor on the character following a mistake, you can replace the character by pressing DEL-left. If you place the cursor over the error, the DEL-right key will delete it. To insert a new character (which might be a space), simply position the cursor and type the character. You can always delete a character easily, so try to work up to as fast a speed as possible. Nothing will be printed on the paper until you press RETURN, so you can make all your corrections, then press RETURN when the text is perfect. If the text starts to look broken up into awkward lines after a correction, press the RELAY key (left of the down-arrow cursor key). This will lay out the text again in a correct form. Remember that the text is not printed until you press RETURN. Once the text has been printed, it vanishes from the screen and is gone for good except for the paper copy.

(a)   This is an example of the PCW8256 used in direct mode, with the left margin set to places.

(b)   This is an example of the PCW8256 used in direct mode, with the left margin set to 8 places.

(c)   This is an example of a longer piece of text which will use several lines. The text is not printed until all of it has been typed, so you need to keep your little finger away from the RETURN key until you have finished. This is not easy, because the RETURN key is large, and you need to use the SHIFT key several times. This is why you need practice with the keyboard before you start word processing.

Figure 2.1. Some examples of direct printing. (a) The effect of using too large a left margin, (b) a better margin choice, (c) illustrating that the RETURN key need not be pressed until the end of a paragraph.

Important note: In direct mode, the most sensible use of the RETURN key is for each paragraph, allowing you to check and correct the text in convenient sized chunks.

Print effects

Even in direct mode, it's useful to be able to carry out tasks like underlining, bold print, italics, and so on. The advantage of trying out these things in direct mode is that it lets you experiment without all the complications of the full word processing system, so that you can find out how to get the print effects that you want quickly and easily. Even when you are accustomed to using the PCW 8256 in word processing mode, you will find it convenient to try out print styles with direct mode now and again. The special effects can be achieved in more than one way, and the various methods will be described here. Direct mode is also very useful for trying out the alternative characters, illustrated in Appendices A, B and C. Figure 2.1 shows the results of some direct printing, including the effect of setting the left margin too far to the right.

To underline text you need to mark the start and the end of the underlining. The marks can be made using the Emphasis menu, which is called up by using key f3. Type the words 'This is an example of', and then press f3. When the menu appears, cancel the tick beside Full underline by using the [–] key, or place the cursor over the Word underline legend and press the [+] key. Press ENTER to confirm. As you type the words 'word underline' you will see the underlining appear on the screen. Following these words, press f3 again, and cancel the underlining by using the [–] key, then ENTER. The rest of the words will then appear with no underlining. Using word underline will make the underline appear only under words, not under spaces, which looks neater. Full underlining makes the underline appear under all characters, including spaces, and should be reserved for extra emphasis.

Another method of calling up and cancelling the underlining, which is quicker to use, is to call up the SET menu when you want to start underlining. This menu is obtained by pressing the [+] key, and waiting for a fraction of a second. If you are in a hurry, you can press the [+] key and then the key that is marked with a criss-cross chequer pattern at the centre of the cursor keys. The cursor on the menu is moved to Word underline, and you press ENTER to confirm. Remember that you can always press CAN to cancel a choice before you press ENTER. To clear the underline, you call up the CLEAR menu by pressing the [–] key, using the criss-cross key also if you are in a hurry. Select underline by moving the cursor, and then press ENTER to clear the underline. You can then continue typing.

The ultimate in speed is obtained by *dispensing with the menu* altogether! This is the method that you should practise, because it can save a great deal of time when you start word processing. When you get to the place where you want to start underlining, press the [+] key followed right away by **W**, and

SET	CLEAR
+	-
Bold	**Bold**
Centre	Double
Double	Italic
Italic	Keep ??
Keep ??	LayouT
LayouT ?	Line Pitch
Line Pitch ?	Line Spacing
Line Spacing ??	Pitch
Last Line	ReVerse
Last Page Number	SuBscript
Pitch ?? ?	SupeRscript
Page Number	UnderLine
ReVerse	(⌣) soft space
Right Justify	(-) soft hyphen
SuBscript	
SupeRscript	
UnderLine	
Word underline	
UniT	
⌣ hard space	
⌢ hard hyphen	

Figure 2.2. The SET and CLEAR menus. The SET menu is obtained using the [+] key, the CLEAR menu with the [-] key.

underlining will start. You end the underlining by pressing the [-] key followed by **UL**. How would you know which letter codes to use? Simple; they are the capital letters in the SET and CLEAR menu examples, and they are listed in Figure 2.2. Not all of these menu choices are important at the moment, and some of the actions need other data to be fed in – we'll leave these at the moment. It's easy enough, however, to try out some of the actions such as underlined print, as in Figure 2.3.

To use bold, italic and double print you can call up the appropriate menus, but it's much easier to use the SET/CLEAR menu, or in the fast and easy method, to use the abbreviations along with the [+] and [-] keys. The bold print style can be a very useful one, because if you select bold print for text, it can give text that is more readable than draft quality, but with much faster printing than the high quality text. You can combine bold with underlining, or double print underlining, or you can have bold italic and double italic; you can even have bold and double together, though it's slow and not all that much clearer than bold. These options are illustrated in Figure 2.5.

To centre a title line, you can call up the **f5** menu, use the SET menu with

(a)   This is an example of word underline in action.

(b)   This uses the SET menu option for underlining.

(c)   This is the ultimate method of underlining, using W and UL only.

Figure 2.3. Underlined printing, with a reminder of the methods that can be used to obtain it.

the cursor placed at Centre, or just type [+]C at the start of the line. This actions centres one line, and there is no need to cancel because the action is automatically applied to one line only, as illustrated in Figure 2.4(a). As the illustration shows, the title can also make use of other codes, and bold has been illustrated. In this case, the key sequence was [+]C[+]B (then the text) [-]B.

To right justify a line, use the f5 menu, select from the SET menu, or use [+]RJ. You don't need any [-]RJ because right justification, like centring, applies to one line only. Right justification does only what the name suggests – it places a line so that the last character is at the right-hand margin, as illustrated in Figure 2.4(b). This is useful for some letters, in which you might want to place a name and address at the right-hand side of the page. It is *not* the same as full justification, in which the words of a line are spaced so as to fill the whole line, making both left and right sides line up on the page. For this option, you need to be able to use the Layout option, and this is covered later in Sections 5, 6 and 7.

This is a Centred Title

(a)

THIS IS A BOLD TITLE

(b)   This text is right justified.

Figure 2.4. (a) Centring text and (b) right justification of text.

This is an example of **bold print** which does not show on screen.

This is an example of *italic print* which also does not show on screen.

This is an example of **double print** which does not show on screen.

By using bold text for all the words in a document, the quality of text is improved, but printing is faster than with high quality selected. You <u>cannot</u> select both high quality and bold.

You can have *bold italic* and *double italic* also.

Using **bold double** gives this.

Figure 2.5. Bold, italic and double print styles illustrated.

To make use of subscripts and superscripts you need the SET and CLEAR menus, or the use of SB and SR, since it's not quite so straightforward to get the appropriate menu from direct print mode. As you progress, you'll probably conclude that the use of these abbreviation command letters is a lot simpler than using the menus in any case. Figure 2.6 shows subscript and

This shows subscript and superscript in use.

Tritium is the isotope $^3T_1$.

$y=3x^2+4x+5$

$\alpha=_1\Sigma ax^n$

$\alpha=_1\Sigma ax^n$
$\alpha=^5\Sigma ax$

Figure 2.6. Using subscript and superscript. These are particularly helpful if you need to work with chemical or mathematical texts.

superscript in use. Note that the print size has been automatically reduced in these modes, so that it's easy to fit text with these effects in normal text. The subscripts and superscripts are particularly useful for a range of scientific and mathematical work, particularly in conjunction with the special symbols that you can get on the keyboard when you press the ALT or EXTRA keys (see Appendices A and B). In the illustration, the phrase 'Tritium is the isotope 3T1' has been printed with the letter strokes [+]SR3[-]SRT[+]SB1[-]SB around the 3T1 section. The shape of the numbers is not particularly good in this typeface, however.

It *is* possible to achieve both a subscript and a superscript in the same column, as the example in Figure 2.7 shows. This has been done by typing the

$\alpha=^5_5\Sigma ax^n$

Figure 2.7. Placing a subscript and a superscript in the same column.

symbols, using [+]SB1[-]SB first time round, then using the SET menu to select line spacing and typing 0 to get a zero line space. When RETURN is pressed, the printer will print the line with the subscript number only, but will not take a new line. You then space over to the position of the subscript, just before the sigma sign, and press [+]SR5[-] to get the superscript 5, then press RETURN again. This puts the superscript 5 into position. It's not the sort of thing you will want to do very often, though! Note that the zero line spacing action lasts only for one press of the RETURN key in this mode.

To type in reverse video, press [+]RV before the word or phrase that you want to show on screen in this mode, and press [-]RV to end the action. Using reverse video makes no difference to what is printed on the paper, but you see the words on the screen in black on green. Some users prefer this appearance. When you are word processing, the use of reverse video can be helpful in drawing your attention to words that might have to be altered in a document, but which must appear normally when printed. This is something that we'll look at again when we deal with layouts in Sections 5, 6 and 7.

To show the selected actions on the screen may sometimes be useful. Of all the effects that we have discussed, only underlining ever shows directly on the screen. Press the **f1** key to bring down the Show state of menu, and with the cursor over Codes, press the [+] key, then ENTER. The [+] key has been used to make the selection, and the ENTER key to confirm that you want to use the selection you have made. The effect of this now is to force the machine to show the hidden codes on the screen, so that the start of bold type is marked with (+Bold) and the end with (— Bold) and so on. The only snag with this is that it upsets the relationship between what you see on the screen and what you get on the printer as far as line layout is concerned, because these words do not, of course, appear on the paper.

Practise now some direct typing of the sort of text you are likely to use. This is particularly important if you are going to use Greek letters for typing formulae, or continental accented letters. For the full range of characters obtainable see Appendices A and B. For typing accented letters see Appendix C.

Section Three
Starting Word Processing

Groups and layouts

When you use your PCW 8256 for word processing, a lot of your documents will require the same fixed layout. If you are writing books, for example, it's likely that you'll want the simplest layout, using A4 paper with double line spacing, and possibly with a chapter title at the top of each page (the header) and a page number at the foot (the footer). If you use the machine for nothing else but this purpose, then this is the one and only layout of text that you will need. It's much more likely, though, that you will want to use paper in many other ways. You might, for example, want to have a layout for letters to close friends. Such a layout would not need much preparation, just your address, a 'Dear Someone' and a 'Yours' at the end. It might be on A4 or on A5 size paper, and it will use single spaced lines, getting as many words to the page as possible, with no page numbering, footers or headers.

You might also want to create some business letters. These would be set out more formally, mostly on A4 paper, with your name and address, the name and address of the person you are writing to, the date, possibly the phrase 'Your Ref:', and ending with a 'Yours sincerely' or 'Yours faithfully' according to whether or not you know the name of the person to whom the letter is addressed. You would also want to have at least one layout for addressing envelopes, most of which will be of the C6 size, but you may also need to address envelopes of C5 or C4 sizes. You may need a layout for simple VAT invoices, with your name, address and VAT registration number, showing goods purchased, amount of VAT and total. You may need a memorandum layout for communication between offices, or a record sheet for a day's work. Whatever the requirements, they are met by using the *group* system of the PCW 8256.

The principle is that you never have to start designing a document absolutely from scratch except when you are trying things for the first time. The LOCO SCRIPT disc keeps documents divided into groups, each group containing documents which are identically, or almost identically, laid out. In each group there is a special file called TEMPLATE.STD. This file contains what is called the 'base layout', meaning the pattern on which you can construct the kind of document that will be stored in that group. You are not confined to this base layout, however. It is a starting point which you can alter as much as you please for an individual document. What it does, providing the TEMPLA-TE.STD file is not altered, is to provide the starting layout for every document in a group. Altering the TEMPLATE.STD will alter the base layout for all documents in that group.

There are eight groups for each disc that you use, numbered 0 to 7. The numbers disappear only when you change the name of the group (using the **f5** key menu). You would do this normally when you wanted to enter something into a new group for the first time. The master disc which you have copied uses only four of the groups, each with a preset layout ready for use. It makes sense, then, to start word processing with one of the existing groups rather than try to lay out a new group for yourself. The master disc and your Start-of-day copy also contain a set of templates that will be useful to you. We'll look at what is involved in laying out a new group later, in Section 5. These layouts, remember, are preserved in the file called TEMPLATE.STD, one of which is contained in each group. Though the name is always the same, TEMPLATE.STD, the data can be different, since it is data for that particular group.

In this section, then, we'll look at how a letter can be typed, using the letter layout provided in Group 0, Drive A. Notice, incidentally, that a 'Drive M' is referred to. This is not a real disc drive, just a part of the memory which can be used for temporary storage and retrieval. Its advantage is that it works much faster than a disc drive. Its disadvantage is that, like any other part of the memory, it loses all of its data when you switch off, or if power is momentarily interrupted. Even an interruption that just causes the room lights to blink will often cause the memory to become scrambled. Until your data is recorded on a disc, it isn't safe. The M drive, as it is called, is particularly useful when we want to assemble a document from several discs, or to transfer a document file from one disc to another. Details of these actions are in Section 13 on Disc management.

To start work on a document, load in LOCO SCRIPT either by switching on and inserting the LOCO SCRIPT Start-of-day copy or, if the machine is already switched on, by pressing SHIFT/EXTRA/EXIT together with the LOCO SCRIPT disc in the drive facing left. This places the LOCO SCRIPT program into the memory and puts the standard layouts into memory. At the same time, certain data is loaded into Drive M. You can now use a separate data disc to hold any text that you write. Remove the LOCO SCRIPT copy and insert a formatted data disc. For formatting, see Figure 1.7. You are now ready to create a document whenever the disc is 'logged in'. To log in the disc, press key **f1**. This will read and write the disc, and you will see the screen display change, showing what is now available. Since this is a new disc, there won't be anything on the Drive A part of the menu, only on Drive M which is the memory. You'll see now that the groups contain only the TEMPLATE files because there are no documents as yet. All of the groups on Drive A are shown as numbers, because there are no names for them. Drive M, the reserved memory, is always unchanged when you change discs. *Each time you change a disc, you must press the* **f1** *key when the replacement disc is in the drive.*

To name and call up Group 0, you need to have a data disc in the drive and the Disc management menu displayed. The cursor will be on Group 0. Press the **f5** key to call up the Rename menu, and move the cursor with the down-arrow key to the 'Rename group' legend. When you move the cursor to this point, you'll see the phrase ticked, so you don't need to use the [+] key, just press ENTER. This brings up another menu section, asking for a name for the group. You are limited to eight characters for this name – LETTERS is a good one to use at this point! When you have pressed ENTER on this, you'll see the Main menu display again, and you may have to move the top cursor with the SHIFT and cursor keys so that it is over the word LETTERS in the section set aside for Drive A. You are now ready to use this group on the new disc.

To prepare for a letter, press the **C** key, with the cursor over LETTERS in Group 0, Drive A. It's important to have the correct drive letter, because if the cursor is on Drive M, the text will be saved in memory only, not on disc. Pressing the **C** key brings up another sub-menu, asking you to give a name for the document. The name that is supplied is DOCUMENT.000. This is the 'default' name, meaning the name that the machine supplies in case you can't think of anything else. The number is automatically incremented (one is added to it) each time you create a document without supplying a name for it, so that the next document creation would bring up DOCUMENT.001 if you had created a DOCUMENT.000 previously. The name DOCUMENT should serve to remind you that the name you supply here can consist of a first part of up to eight characters, a full-stop, and an 'extension' of up to three characters. The extension letters or digits can be chosen to help you remember what type of letter this is. You could, for example, use **.PRI** to mean private letter, or **.BUS** to mean business letter, or you could simply use numbers. The main name should also be a helpful one. If this is a letter to your friend Jim, then you could use the title JIM   .PRI, or JIM.001 if this is the first letter using the word processor. You aren't *forced* to do all this naming, but it's there to make things easier for you. At first it may look a bit over the top, but when you have several hundred letters on file, you'll see the advantages of being able to use the titles to tell them apart. You could, for example, use the extension space to put month names, like JAN, FEB, MAR and so on to be able to select letters that were written at definite periods.

To select the letter, type the name as above, and press ENTER. You were given the choice of changing group and drive in the previous menu, but you wouldn't normally do so – the facility is there is you ever need it. The screen display now shows a skeleton layout for a letter, with spaces for your address, date, the addressee (the one you are writing to) and the word 'Dear' to start the letter. This is what is meant by the 'template' for the letter. You can, later, change this template so that instead of the words 'your address' it contains your actual address. For the moment, though, we'll use it as it exists. This is the most difficult part of word processing to start with, because it involves using the cursor, delete and TAB keys in a way that was not necessary for direct printing. The effect of pressing the TAB key is indicated by the arrows in the top letter line, directly underneath the green block which reminds you of what has been set up. The first five TAB positions are set out every four spaces, and the final TAB is to position 60. This top line is called the ruler line, and you don't place any text on it; it is used purely as a guide. The ruler positions indicate tenths of an inch steps across the paper, and only the whole inch numbers are shown. Each space or blank in this template is indicated by a dot to make positioning characters easier, but you can have templates in which these dots are omitted if you like. You can also opt to change this feature in this document, using the menu obtained when you press **f1**.

To type your address, press the right cursor key (marked with a right-arrow) until the small cursor reaches the letter 'y' of 'your address' in the template. The small cursor blinks rapidly as it is moved, and you'll find it easier to watch the one above it, on the ruler line, stopping when it reaches the arrow mark for the TAB at position 60. Now use the DEL-right key to remove the words 'your address'. Figure 3.1 shows the steps of this, until the last 's' has been

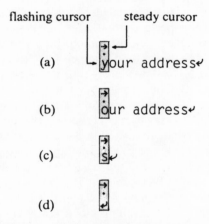

Figure 3.1. The steps that are required to delete a line, using simple editing.

removed. This leaves only the 'curly arrow' which is the symbol for RETURN. At this point, the printer will be forced to take a new line, so the curly arrow mark is important. If you have held down the DEL-right key too long, or pressed it too many times, you may have removed the curly arrow as well, in which case, just type another one by using the RETURN key – you will then have to use the cursor keys to get back in place.

You can now type the first line of your own address. At the end of this line, pressing RETURN will put in the curly arrow, and the cursor will now be at the start of the next line. Use the TAB key to get to the correct position of the next line of the address, and type this line, pressing RETURN at the end of the line. Continue in this way until you have completed the address. You can also fill in the date using this same method. If you find that you have pressed RETURN one more time than you need, and that this creates too many blank lines, just remove one by putting the cursor over the curly arrow and pressing DEL-right. You can also, of course, place the cursor just to the right of the curly arrow and press DEL-left. Filling in the addressee name is easier because no TABs are needed. You can then position the cursor following 'Dear' and type the name. Press RETURN to take a new line after this, space or TAB over to where you want to start, and type your letter. You will probably want to put the 'Yours' or 'Yours sincerely' at the TAB 60 position at the end of the letter.

At this point, don't worry about any misspellings or other problems. The important thing is to make a recording so that this document is placed on the disc as soon as possible. Remember that until a document is recorded on disc, it can be wiped from the memory by any interruption of the power supply. We'll look later, in Section 10, at how you can replace phrases like 'your address' with your own address without all the hassle of deleting the phrase and placing the new text on the screen. This type of action requires the use of the EXCH key, and rather more experience of word processing that you have at the moment.

To record a document, press the EXIT key. You will get a sub-menu in which the cursor is over the legend 'Finish editing', with a tick beside this. Press ENTER on this, and your document will be recorded. The machine then returns to the Main menu, and you can see your letter recorded under its correct title in the Group 0 column. If your letter needs correction, then you can still recover it from the disc and correct it by using the **E** key when the cursor is over the filename of your letter.

It's usually better, however, if the document contains mistakes, to use the 'Save and Continue' option. This saves a copy on the disc, in case of power failure, but keeps the screen copy (in the memory) so that you can work on it and improve it. The 'Save and Print' option saves the document on the disc and prints it, if the printer is ready. It's often easier to check for errors on a printed page than on the screen. The 'Abandon edit' option is used if you have

---

1. Cursor keys are marked with arrows that represent the direction of movement.
2. The cursor can be moved to any part of the document with no effect on text.
3. Wherever the cursor is place, a character can be inserted.
4. The DEL key with the left-arrow will delete the character to the left of the cursor.
5. The DEL key with the right-arrow will delete the character under the cursor.

Figure 3.2. A summary of the simple editing actions.

decided that you don't want to make the changes after all, and you will keep the previous version of the file on the disc.

To carry out simple editing of a document you need to have it available on the screen. If you have used the Save and Continue option, then your text will still be visible on the screen. If you have simply used the 'Finish editing' option, then the file will not be on screen. Either option will still have saved the file on the disc, unless the disc was write-protected or not placed into the drive. If the file is not on screen, then reload it by using the **E** key. As usual, this brings up the sub-menu for you to confirm that this is the correct file by pressing ENTER. With the file on screen, you can now start editing. Editing is very well described in the manual, and only a summary will be given here, in Figure 3.2. The points to note are:

- What you see on screen is very close to what you get on paper – but remember that the screen shows only 28 lines at a time. Using the TEMPLATE provided for letters allows for 54 single spaced lines per page – suitable for A4 paper. If you type more lines, you will see a thick line inserted to mark the page break. The 'header' in the green strip at the top of the screen shows the page number and the line number at the right-hand side of its middle line.
- You can move one page at a time by using the PAGE key to move down and ALT PAGE to move up.
- Each time an editing operation leaves the text looking ragged, you can restore order by pressing the RELAY key. The RELAY action takes time, particularly on a long document, and its better to carry out all the obvious edit actions, like spelling corrections, before you use RELAY. Always make sure that you have used RELAY before you stop editing.

  Important note: Sometimes the use of RELAY can cause the machine to 'lock up', leaving the keyboard ineffective. The only way out of this is to remove the disc, switch off, then start again. If you did not have your work recorded on the disc, it will be lost. The RELAY action that you must avoid is deleting a piece of text for more than one line, and then pressing RELAY.

- Look at each word carefully. It's much easier to pass over a misspelling or an incorrect word on the screen than on paper. For long documents, always print out a draft version, preferably double spaced, and make your corrections on that. You can then call up the document for editing and put in the corrections. Only the final perfect version should be printed in high quality, because this is very time consuming. A good compromise is to use draft quality and bold type unless the work needs to look particularly good. Remember that high quality on this printer takes longer than on most daisywheel printers! Each time you edit a document the latest version will be recorded, unless you use the 'Abandon edit' option.
- Don't panic! You know that you have a copy of the document on disc

```
                                           22 The Plinge,
                                           Newton Beans,
                                           Worst,
                                           22nd, Feb, 1986
```

Jimmy Jervis,
Olton.

Dear Jim,

See you, Jimmy! I didn't get back until <u>very</u> late last night,
thanks to you rabbiting on about computers. As usual, though, the train
was late (not cancelled this time, thank goodness) and I caught it, I
have decided to take your advice, and buy this new Amstrad machine.
Could you just remind me of what it's called again? I can only remember
it being called the Joyce, and our local shop swore blind that they have
never heard of such a thing.

                                           Cheers,

                                           Tommy.

Figure 3.3. A letter in draft form, using the letter template that is provided.

22 The Plinge,
Newton Beans,
Worst.
22nd. Feb. 1986

Jimmy Jervis,
Olton.

Dear Jim,

    See you, Jimmy! I didn't get back until <u>very</u> late last night, thanks to you rabbiting on about computers. As usual, though, the train was late (not cancelled this time, thank goodness) and I caught it. I have decided to take your advice, and buy this new Amstrad machine. Could you just remind me of what it's called again? I can only remember it being called the Joyce, and our local shop swore blind that they have never heard of such a thing.

                    Cheers,

                        Tommy.

Figure 3.4. The same letter, this time in high quality print style.

already, so if you've got yourself into a complete tangle on editing, you can always abandon the edit and start again. Even if you have recorded an unsatisfactory version, it's always useful. If you have somehow managed to record a badly edited version and so wipe the previous (better) version, you still haven't lost the older one completely. It has become a 'limbo file' and can be recovered by renaming it (see later, Section 13 on Disc management).

● Finally, your disc can have a title. You can do this by pressing the **f5** key when the Disc management menu is showing. Move the cursor down to the 'rename Disc' legend, then press ENTER. You will be prompted for a name of up to eight characters for the disc (such as WP001), and this will be placed on the disc when you press ENTER.

Finally, Figure 3.3 shows a document which has been prepared using the letter template. This letter has been printed using the draft printing style, so that it can be checked more easily for mistakes. The final version, printed in high quality, is shown in Figure 3.4.

Section Four
Printing a Letter

In this section, we'll look at how a letter, such as the sample that was produced in the previous section, is printed. The printing can be carried out in several different ways. Following editing, a document can be printed using the 'Save and Print' option when EXIT has been pressed. You must already have paper loaded into the printer if you want to use this option. If the printer is not ready, the file will be saved but not printed. You can, however, carry out the printing by loading in paper and pressing EXIT. If you have the document on disc, and you don't need to look at it before you print it; simply load paper into the printer and press the **P** key to start the printing. If the document consists of several pages, the paging action will suspend the printing at the end of each page, and printing will not restart until you load another sheet into the printer. When this is done, the Printer menu shows at the top of the green header strip, and you cannot resume printing until you have pressed EXIT to get back to the normal menu in this strip. This allows you to alter some printing actions if you want to before continuing with the printout.

To alter print actions, call up the Printer menu by pressing PTR, or by loading a sheet of paper into the printer. You will see the word 'Printer' flashing on the left-hand side of the second line of the header strip. On the rest of this line, you will see the features that have been set up on the printer. The normal conditions in this state are Online, Top of form, Idle, High quality and Single sheet. The Online message means that the printer is ready to print. This message can be reversed by pressing the **f8** key. If the printer is offline, it cannot print, so if you use the Save and Print option, you will get a message immediately after saving to the effect that printing is impossible. If you now switch the printer online, using **f8** and pressing EXIT, the printing will start normally. Printing will also be impossible if the printer is set for single sheet operation, and you have come to the end of a sheet.

The Top of Form message means that the paper is at its top position. If several lines have been printed already, the line position (numbered from top to bottom) will be shown in this part of the information strip.

To move down the paper, select the 'Actions' menu with **f3**, and check that the cursor is over 'Feed one line'. Pressing the [+] key will cause one line feed, but will keep the menu in place. You can therefore use this to space down the paper, with the result recorded on the header. Do this only if the document that you are printing uses fewer than the normal number of lines (54 printed lines on an A4 sheet, for example). If you simply turn the roller of the printer by hand, you will move the paper, but this movement will not be counted on the header line, and this could cause the printer to print in the wrong lines subsequently. To leave this menu, press ENTER or CAN. Neither of these keys will cause a line feed.

Idle means that the printer is not working, not printing a document nor suspended, waiting for some adjustment. This is an important message, because if the printer has stopped, you need to know whether this is because it has finished printing or because of some other reason, such as a change that has not been confirmed. The printer will not, for example, continue printing after a paper load unless there is more text to print and EXIT has been pressed, with no sub-menus showing.

High quality and Single sheet can be taken together because they are both altered by the same menu. High quality is normally selected for the letter template, and is a good-looking typeface which prints very slowly. For anything but the best work, then, you should select Draft quality. This is done by pressing the **f1** key with the Printer menu showing. The change can be made either by pressing the [−] key when the cursor is over High quality, or by shifting the cursor to Draft quality and pressing the [+] key. Pressing ENTER confirms the choice. Figure 4.1 shows a brief letter which has used the template, and which is printed using Draft quality. In the same menu, you can also choose single sheet paper or continuous stationery. Use the continuous option only if you are using computer stationery of the fanfold or teletype roll variety − if you are doing this you will probably have to make several other changes, because a lot of continuous stationery is not in A4 size sheets. The simplest type of continuous stationery is the 'teletype roll', a roll of plain paper which will need a roll holder (not supplied with the PWC 8256). The most awkward paper to use is the fanfold type, which is perforated to allow easy separation. Unless the printer has been correctly set up, you may find that the pages start to print over the perforations. In addition, you will need to use the tractor feed attachment which is supplied with the package. Use of this type of paper is dealt with in Section 12.

Text options

We shall look now at some of the options which can be selected, other than setting up for a new paper size. All of the options described here are selected, when you are creating or editing a document, with the strip on the top of the screen showing the words 'Editing text' just following the document name at the top left.

To alter print style, press **f4** to bring up the Character style menu. This menu offers the choice of half height, italic, and different pitch numbers. If you

```
                                "Rosy Glow",
                                Gin Lane,
                                Distilbury,
                                Hiccs

                                23rd, March, 1986




Florry Barbender,
27 The Swill,
Rumdoo,
Perks.

Dear Florrie,

      Your welcome letter was really a surprise to me
after all these years. I suggest that the best thing to do
is to get together at the old haunt, the Stuck Pig at
Whistlethorpe. How about Tuesday at 7.00 p.m.? If you have a
phone, could you give me a bell to confirm?

                                Yours,

                                Jim.
```

Figure 4.1. An example of a letter using draft quality, 10-pitch.

```
                              "Rosy Glow",
                              Gin Lane,
                              Distilbury,
                              Hiccs

                        23rd. March, 1986

Florry Barbender,
27 The Swill,
Rumdoo,
Perks.

Dear Florrie,

     Your welcome letter was really a surprise to me after all
these years. I suggest that the best thing to do is to get together at
the old haunt, the Stuck Pig at Whistlethorpe. How about Tuesday at 7.00
p.m.? If you have a phone, give me a bell to confirm?

                              Yours,

                              Jim.
```

Figure 4.2. The same letter in subscript.

"Rosy Glow",
Gin Lane,
Distilbury,
Hiccs

23rd, March, 1986

Florry Barbender,
27 The Swill,
Rumdoo,
Perks.

Dear Florrie,

Your welcome letter was really a surprise to me after all these years. I suggest that the best thing to do is to get together at the old haunt, the Stuck Pig at Whistlethorpe. How about Tuesday at 7.00 p.m.? If you have a phone, could you give me a bell to confirm?

Yours,

Jim.

Figure 4.3. Italic printing considerably alters the appearance of the letter.

```
                                        "Rosy Glow",
                                        Gin Lane,
                                        Distilbury,
                                        Hiccs

                                        23rd. March, 1986
```

```
Florry Barbender,
27 The Swill,
Rumdoo,
Perks.

Dear Florrie,

        Your welcome letter was really a surprise to me after all these years. I
suggest that the best thing to do is to get together at the old haunt, the Stuck Pig at
Whistlethorpe. How about Tuesday at 7.00 p.m.? If you have a phone, could you give me a
bell to confirm?

                                        Yours,

                                        Jim.
```

Figure 4.4. The use of 15-pitch for a letter allows a considerably greater number of words per line.

choose half height or pitch number change, the menu will be extended to allow further choice. Starting with half height, which is the one that the cursor will normally be over, this gives reduced height characters. If you take this option by pressing the [+] key, you will then be given the further choice of subscript or superscript. These are the same choices as you had in the SET menu, but in this case they can be applied to the whole of the text. If you choose subscript with the [+] key (then ENTER), this will put the SUB code at the start of the text. You could have achieved the same effect, in other words, simply by using the [+]SB code at the start of the letter. Figure 4.2 shows the effect, and Figure 4.3 shows the effect of selecting italic. This effect also could just as easily have been obtained by putting in the code at the start of the document. These effects, like pitch selection (following) do not show on the screen. It's a good idea, then, once you have finished the editing of a letter to get it into the right shape, to display the codes (use **f1** menu) so that next time you want to use this letter you can see what typestyle was used.

To change the pitch of printing select the **f4** menu while editing. Move the cursor down to the 'Pitch' legend, and press the [+] key. Now use the extended menu to select the 10-pitch setting, and press ENTER. You will see that the effect is the same as using [+]P10, waiting for the confirmation in a menu at the right-hand side, and then pressing ENTER. Figure 4.1 illustrated 10-pitch, and Figure 4.4 shows the effect of printing in 15-pitch. The pitch means the number of characters per inch, so that the lower the pitch number, the smaller the characters.

Each selection can be made in either of the ways described above. When you move to a different pitch, your letter layout will alter in the sense that you will get more words per line. The margins, tab stops and other features, however, have been determined by the base layout in TEMPLATE.STD, and *are not altered* when you change the pitch in this way. These settings need to be changed to allow for a print size change only if you are changing the print size in the layout.

Another choice from this group is proportional spacing, which gives 12-pitch, but with the spacing between characters altered to suit the widths of the characters. This is not possible on normal electric typewriters, which keep a constant space between letters. Proportional spacing is hardly worth using with draft quality, but when this is combined with high quality print, the effect is very impressive as Figure 4.5 shows. You cannot select proportional spacing along with any pitch other than 12-pitch. The abbreviation to use with the [+] key is PPS.

You can also select double width printing, which can give a very distinctive appearance, illustrated in Figure 4.6. This type of text is very useful for headings when you combine it with 10-pitch. When you leave the Editing menu to print after selecting double width, you will notice the text on the screen rearranging itself. This is because the former arrangement was unsuitable, since only half the number of characters can now be printed in each line. It's as if you had pressed the RELAY key, and you would see the

```
                            "Rosy Glow",
                            Gin Lane,
                            Distilbury,
                            Hiccs

                            23rd. March, 1986


Florry Barbender,
27 The Swill,
Rumdoo,
Perks.

Dear Florrie,

        Your welcome letter was really a surprise to me after all
these years. I suggest that the best thing to do is to get together at the
old haunt, the Stuck Pig at Whistlethorpe. How about Tuesday at 7.00 p.m.?
If you have a phone, could you give me a bell to confirm?

                                            Yours,

                                            Jim.
```

Figure 4.5. Using proportional spacing makes the letter appear printed rather than typed.

```
                                    "Rosy Glow",
                                    Gin Lane,
                                    Distilbury,
                                    Hiccs

                                    23rd. March,
1986

Florry Barbender,
27 The Swill,
Rumdoo,
Perks.

Dear Florrie,
          Your welcome letter was really a
surprise to me after all these years. I
suggest that the best thing to do is to get
together at the old haunt, the Stuck Pig at
Whistlethorpe. How about Tuesday at 7.00
p.m.? If you have a phone, could you give me
a bell to confirm?

                                    Yours,
                                      Jim.
```

Figure 4.6. Double width is more useful for headings, but it can be used for letters as this shows.

same effect if you pressed the RELAY key before printing. There is no other indication on the screen that you are printing in double width, and you will once again be able to see the selection codes appear if you have taken this option.

Using print styles

Since the use of an ordinary typewriter does not allow you much choice of typestyles, you need to experiment to some extent with this new found freedom in order to see how you would use it. The following list is by no means exhaustive, but some of the suggestions may be useful to you.

- Headings can use underlining, bold face, or double width 10-pitch. For a company name on a letterhead, double width 10-pitch is particularly suitable.
- Personal letters can use 15-pitch or 12-pitch in order to fit more words onto the page. Using bold print gives a better-looking text, and is much faster than using high quality.
- If a letter contains a quotation from another document, this can be highlighted very effectively by putting it in smaller type, such as 15-pitch bold, and using larger margins. An example will be shown in Section 7.
- If the text you are using contains accented letters, or letters from the ALT or EXTRA set (see Appendices A and B), then it's better to use a bold type because these marks are not easily visible in draft quality.
- Using a fine pitch in double width can be very eyecatching.
- Italic type is a very useful way of highlighting something different, such as a footnote, and can be combined with other options of size and width. You can also use italic bold, normal or double width.

Section Five
New Layouts

The letter layout which we looked at in the two previous sections was suitable for simple letters on A4 paper. In this section we shall look at how new layout templates can be created, so that you can design templates for other uses, such as business letters, reports, envelopes and VAT invoices. Before we start, though, some information on paper sizes and on how distances are specified may be useful. The most difficult part of any new template is to get the margins correct, and Figure 5.1a shows the sizes of the metric paper standards for A4, A5 and the envelope C6, C5 and C4 standards. Figure 5.1b shows the alternative continuous stationery sizes, both for perforated and unperforated paper, all in units of tenths of an inch which the PCW 8256 requires. If you do not know the thinking behind the metric paper dimensions, the idea is that A0 is one square metre in area, with sides approximately 1188×840 mm in size. The A1 size is obtained by cutting the A0 sheet halfway along its longer side, to obtain a sheet of 840×594 mm, and this in turn can be halved to get the A2 sheet. This makes the A4 sheet 297 mm $\times$ 210 mm. A5 is a small letter and memo size, which fits with one fold into the C6 envelopes. A4 is for larger letters and reports. It can be fitted into a C6 envelope with two folds, or can be put in C5 (one fold) or C4 envelopes (unfolded). The A3 size and larger are used mainly for drawings. The printer of the PCW 8256 will not accept A3 paper, unlike most office daisywheel printers.

The importance of these sizes is that they have to be used in the design work of setting up a template. The examples in this section illustrate a few useful templates, but it's essential to be able to design these for yourself so that you can cope with odd sizes, and with various pre-printed forms and other material. In this section, we shall look in detail at the design of a template for a very simple (and not very elegant) A5 VAT form, and show the template information for a business letter, a report, and a C6 envelope. One very important point to remember, however, is that the numbers which are used on the screen and on the printer correspond to the standard size of text, meaning ten characters per inch, and different numbers will need to be used if you opt for a different size of text lettering. 'What you see is what you get' applies only to the standard settings! You will have to learn by experience how to interpret what you see on the screen when your base layout uses, for example, 15-pitch

(a)

PAPER SIZES
(single sheet)

A4

117

83

A5

83

58

ENVELOPE SIZES

C6

45

64

C5

90

64

C4

128

90

All dimensions in tenths

Figure 5.1. Paper sizes. (a) The A4 and A5 paper sizes, with C6, C5 and C4 envelope sizes. All dimensions are in $1/10$ inch units as required for setting up layouts. (b) Continuous paper styles.

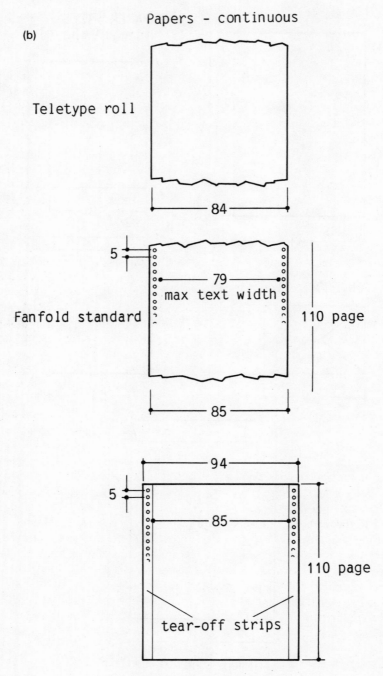

Figure 5.1. cont.

lettering. Because the normal screen width is only 90 characters wide, you have to see the right-hand side of wider documents by scrolling sideways, using the right-arrow cursor key. If you are using the full width of A4 with 15 or 17-pitch characters, you will not normally see the whole of one line at a time. Unless you have to use such fine pitch in A4 for some special reason, then, I suggest that you keep to 10 or 12-pitch for A4, and use 15 or 17-pitch full-width for A5 paper. An obvious exception is where you might want to place an inset section of 15-pitch into an A4 document, since the base layout will determine the real width.

To pick a group for a new base layout template, choose a group number that is free for use. On your data disc so far, you will have used only Group 0, leaving the other seven groups free. Use the cursor to select a group and then press the **f5** key, which allows renaming. By shifting the cursor and typing, you can name the group and the document. For this example, we can name the group as SMALLVAT, and the initial document (later) as VAT.001. When the cursor is over 'rename Group', press the ENTER key. This produces another sub-menu, with the cursor placed so that you can type the name of this group. When the name has been typed, pressing ENTER will fix it in place on the disc and in the Main menu. You can now set up a template for this group. Obviously, if there is a template on the LOCO SCRIPT copy disc, you can use this by copying the TEMPLATE.STD from the LOCO SCRIPT disc into memory (Drive M) and then to your data disc. Details of this type of action are given in Section 13, Disc management.

To start a layout, position the cursor over your new group (it will probably be in place anyway), and press the C key, just as if you were about to create another document. When the sub-menu appears, type the name for your document, TEMPLATE.STD since this is a new template. When you press ENTER, you will probably see the letter template, since this is the only one on the data disc. If you are using the LOCO SCRIPT disc, you may see some other template. At this point, ignore what you see, checking only that the group name and template name are displayed at the top left-hand corner. Now press key **f7**, marked 'Modes'. The first choice on this menu is 'Edit header', and this is the option to take by pressing ENTER. When you press ENTER, the screen layout will change again to show a layout for the headers and footers of pages. This is not what you want at the moment, but there is now a new set of f-key options, and the one to press is once again **f7**. This clears the layout, showing the 'default' layout for A4. You are now ready to specify your layout for the A5 paper which you intend to use.

To set the left margin, you should first of all insert a piece of A5 paper in the printer, and centre it. You'll see that the paper is centred when the edges fall on (or close to) the 10 and 70 marks on the printer bail bar. These positions on the printer correspond to the 10 and 70 positions on the screen also. For an A5 form, small margins of around 5 units are acceptable, so we need to set the left margin at 15. These choices, remember, apply only if you intend to use the 10 characters per inch setting. Make sure that the choices on the green strip start with 'f1 = Options'. If this is not what is displayed, press the EXIT key to get to the correct set, the **Editing base layout** set. Now press **f1** to bring up yet another set of f-key options. Bring the cursor down with the down-arrow key, and move the cursor right to position 15. Now press the **f1** key, and you will see the margin move to this point. The left margin is now set.

To set the right margin, stay in the Editing base layout set, or return to it if you have left it. Move the cursor to the 65 position, and press the **f2** key. This, as you can see, sets the right margin. The next step is to reset the tab stops.

To reset the tab stops, you may want to clear all the existing tabs. To do so, move the cursor to each tab arrow, and press the [–] key to remove the tab. You can now insert tabs where you like by using the cursor and f-keys 3 to 6. A useful point for an ordinary tab is position 20, which is suitable for indenting the start of a paragraph. Move the cursor to this point, and press the **f3** key to put in the tab stop. For the other tabs, it may be useful to make use of some of the different types of tab. The centre tab (key **f5**) will place text so that it is centred, and the position for this is 40. Once again, the cursor is moved to this point, and key **f5** is pressed. Figure 5.2 shows how this figure

---

1. Add margin numbers. In this example, $10 + 70 = 80$.
2. Take half of this number, which will be the centre position. In this example, $80/2 = 40$.

Figure 5.2. Calculating the centre position from the margin settings.

is obtained. The right tab will cause text to be lined up against the right-tab position, and the decimal tab will line up money (or other) figures so that the decimal points are vertically aligned. For our sample document, place the decimal tab (key **f6**) at 45 and the right tab (key **f4**) at 60.

To set other features of layout, move the cursor up to the middle line of the green band again. You will see Pitch 12 highlighted. For A5, it's preferable to use a smaller type size. The next size down is 15, but using this will *totally* upset all our numbered positions. This time, we'll play safe, and go for 10-pitch, which will ensure that we get something similar to what we see. Type 10, and press ENTER to confirm. If, incidentally, you press the [+] key after typing '10', then the letter 'D' will appear, to indicate double width. Press the [–] key to remove this. When you have pressed ENTER on this choice, you can move the cursor right to the line pitch choice. The line pitch figure is the number of lines per vertical inch, and for the spacing of print we shall use, 8-pitch is better. We would certainly want to use 8-pitch if we had chosen to use the 15-pitch type size, otherwise the lines would appear to have a very large blank space between them. The choice is only between 6 and 8, so type 8 and press ENTER.

The next option is Line space. In this example, you need the existing spacing of one line, so that this choice is left undisturbed. The remaining two choices, Italic and Justify, are unavailable unless you see a tick against them. To put in the tick, position the cursor over the word, then press the [+] key. To remove an existing tick, use the [-] key. For the example here, neither italics nor justification is needed, and you can now press EXIT to leave the Edit base layout menu system.

You are now in the ordinary header layout menu. If your VAT documents are for UK purposes, you will need to use an ordinary decimal point, and you probably want the ordinary style of zero. Using the slashed zero, which is de rigueur for computer listing, can cause confusion with the digit 8 in ordinary letters. Changes here are catered for by pressing f3, which allows you to specify a comma as a decimal indicator (for continental invoices), or the slashed zero. Neither is needed for this example, and if you have brought up this menu to see what it looks like, you can cancel it by pressing the CAN key. You should, however, use the f5 key to get the layout and tab count menu. This menu allows you to specify how many changes of layout you will want to make in the document, and how many tab settings you will need in each layout. Each can be set up to a maximum of 99, but you will usually find a more sensible 'default' pair of figures. Using more than you will ever need is a waste of disc space, so we'll specify one change of layout and just five tabs each. As usual, the specification is done by positioning the cursor, typing the new figure and pressing ENTER. If you have put in five tabs on the layout, and you then opt for a smaller number at this stage, all of your tabs will disappear later! When you have made your choice of layout changes and tabs, a final 'ENTER' confirms the choices and returns you to the normal display. You can now look at the f6 menu, and then press the CAN key. All of our VAT forms will be one page long, so page breaking is of no concern here. The next choice of page size (f7) is, however, of very considerable concern.

To set the page size, call up the sub-menu. The default settings will be shown, and for A4 paper these start with a page length of 70. This means that a page that was completely printed would contain 70 lines. The dimension is in terms of the usual figure of six lines per inch, and the figure is obtained by multiplying the depth of the paper in inches by 6. With A4, this works out to $11.7 \times 6 = 70.2$, so 70 is the number that we use, ignoring fractions of a line. This will not apply to our A5 page, so we have to calculate what is needed. At 8 lines per inch, and a vertical distance of 8.3 inches, we can get in $8.3 \times 8 = 66.4$ lines, which we round down to 66. For Page length, then, we type 66, and press ENTER. This will cause the 'page body' figure to change, because this number is the actual number of lines that will be printed. We now have to set the sizes of the header and footer zones, the top and bottom parts of the page. For this form, we shall print INVOICE in the header and E & OE (Errors and Omissions Excepted) in the footer.

To position header and footer, move the cursor to the 'Header zone' legend. Now you can't just put in any old figure here. If you look at the A5 sheet

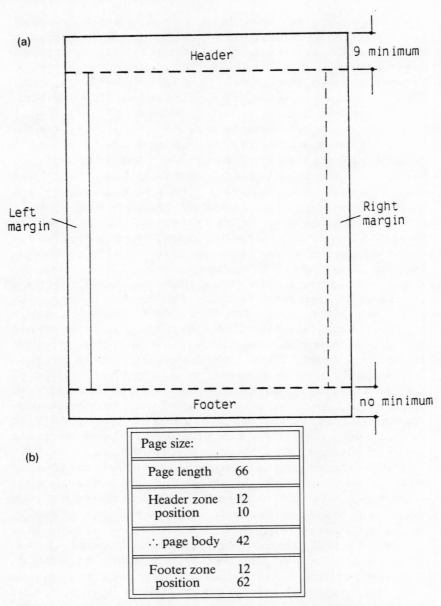

Figure 5.3. (a) The page size display, with (b) settings for A4.

sitting in the printer, you'll see that the printhead is about an inch below the top of the paper. Even if you put in no header at all, then, the printing will start this far down. One inch corresponds to 8 lines, so we really need to make the header zone bigger than this, perhaps 12 lines. Type 12 and press ENTER. We can put in the header at line 10, so move the cursor down, type 10 for 'position', and press ENTER. Now move the cursor to the Footer zone legend. An equal size of footer seems reasonable, so type 12 here, press ENTER, and move down to footer position. With 66 lines available, line 62 seems a reasonable position for it and this also can be entered. You should now see the display as in Figure 5.3(b). If the choices that you make when editing your own layout are impossible, you will be reminded of this by the warning message 'inconsistent' in the 'page body' box. When you have finished entering numbers in this menu, press ENTER to return to the editing page.

The last set of options is called up by the **f8** key, and concerns page numbering (called 'pagination') and the choices of header and footer messages on different pages. For this type of document, the choices that are already ticked (All pages same, Headers and Footers enabled) will suffice, and we can CANcel this menu. Now use EXIT to leave the header editing section, and press ENTER to confirm this when the Confirm/Cancel choice appears. This gets you to the header/footer editing screen.

To enter the header, press the **f5** key to get the Lines menu, and press the [+] C keys for centring. Now type the word INVOICE, and press RETURN. Move the cursor down to the blank line above 'end of footer 1', use the centre instruction again, then type E&OE, and press RETURN. The other two lines, for second header and footer, are not used because we chose not to have different headers and footers on different pages.

You can now leave the header editing, and return to the Main menu, using EXIT and then ENTER. So far, nothing much seems to have been achieved, because the menu only shows this header as the document TEMPLATE.STD so far. What we need to do now is put in anything that we need. This is done in the ordinary way, using the E option, and the result is shown in Figure 5.4.

The next step is to make some use of this template to print a document. It is at this point that you may start to doubt either your sanity or the manual. Everything goes reasonably smoothly until you try to use these decimal and centre tabs. With the V1.1 of LOCO SCRIPT, if you do as is indicated in the manual on page 76, you'll see that the only tab positions recognised are the one five spaces in and the one at the right-hand side. To get the decimal tab to work on this layout with my version of LOCO SCRIPT, it was necessary to use the spacebar to place the cursor somewhere between the centre tab and the decimal tab, and then type the amount. This did *not* align on the screen, but as Figure 5.5 shows, it did align correctly on the paper. The action is perfectly normal, as per the manual, if the centre tab is removed. Another feature of my machine was that the centre tab effect worked only when ALT TAB was used, rather than an ordinary TAB. The effect, however, was an ordinary tab stop rather than centring text, as the manual implied. Incidentally, trying to use the centre, decimal and right tabs when setting up the layout was also ineffective, and pressing the RELAY key caused the machine to lock up completely, with no keys effective. It's at times like that you are glad that you saved everything on disc (didn't you?). No doubt it will

```
                        INVOICE

        Bitslice & Hack,
        Unit 317,
        Mildew Ind. Est.,
        Chipstow,
        Silts.                      Tel:Chip 23477

            Purveyers of fine quality software



GOODS

VAT

TOTAL


To:  Addressee
```

Figure 5.4. The simple VAT invoice template.

all be sorted out by the time later versions of LOCO SCRIPT are available. At the time of writing, version 1.3 was reported to be available, and the older versions, such as my V1.1, can probably be exchanged.

From all this, you might easily gather that making a new layout is sheer

```
                    INVOICE

       Bitslice & Hack,
       Unit 317,
       Mildew Ind. Est.,
       Chipstow,
       Silts.                 Tel:Chip 23477

       30th. March, 1986
          Purveyers of fine quality software

       Spelling checker V2211/23

GOODS:                  £220.00

VAT                     £33.00

TOTAL                   £253.00


To: The Ever-hopeful Co.,
    10 Knee Trembling,
    Hardly Doubtful
    Suffolk.












                    E&OE
```

Figure 5.5. The invoice in use, with details filled in.

hell. It is, but you should only have to do it once for each new layout you might use, and from then on it's automatic. I should mention that I think LOCO SCRIPT is certainly more difficult to use (and more troublesome) in this respect than any of the other word processors I have used, but these were on rather more expensive machines. A new program, which LOCO SCRIPT is, always has teething troubles, and provided you are meticulous about saving your work on disc, and you take care of your discs, things like incorrect layouts and lock ups should not cause too much loss of time. When the program is fully sorted out, there should never be a lock up under any circumstances – certainly this has been my experience with other modestly-priced word processors.

An envelope layout

Envelopes, particularly in the small C6 size, are the most awkward items that can be offered to the printer of a word processor, or indeed to a typewriter. For one thing, the C6 envelope is small, and not much of it is in contact with the rollers of the printer except when the typehead is over the middle of the envelope. For another thing, the thickness of the envelope varies because of the folded-over sections, and this also can cause the grip of the printer to become rather uncertain. Because of this you may find that an envelope will start to load into the printer, but will stick before the top of the envelope reaches the printhead. Another common problem is that the envelope alters angle as it loads in, ending up crooked. Even worse is the situation in which the envelope loads into the printer, but refuses to line feed evenly, so that the address is badly printed, with one line on top of another, or printed at different angles. One solution to the loading problem is to load all envelopes manually, pressing the envelope in with one hand and winding the roller with the other. Another solution, the one I favour, is to load the envelope in the conventional way, but with the left-hand edge of the envelope hard against the left-hand side of the inside of the printer casing. If the envelope is helped into place with a slight push as it loads, it will end up in the correct position, and the guidance of the printer casing prevents the envelope from skewing round. The two small paper rollers on the bail bar should be moved to the left so that one is in contact with each side of the envelope. This last step helps to keep the envelope line feeding correctly, though if you attempt to print too close to the bottom of the envelope you will inevitably have trouble with line feeding.

All of this makes it sound rather more trouble than it's worth, but the use of a word processor for envelopes can be very worthwhile indeed. Even though the Amstrad printer on the PCW 8256 is not ideally suited for envelopes (few printers are, though some daisywheel types can feed envelopes very smoothly), the use of the PCW 8256 for envelopes can bring several benefits. This is particularly true if a whole set of envelopes has to be addressed in one session. For example, if you have to mail reports to the same set of 50 names and addresses each week or each month, the sheer labour of addressing envelopes with a conventional typewriter is quite formidable. In such an example, the list of names and addresses can be held as a file, with a 'new page' code following each address, and the file printed out on the envelopes as needed. Because the list is held as a word processing file, it's easy to modify when you need to add new names or delete old ones. Using such a file, you can concentrate on loading the envelopes, knowing that each address will be printed when you press the EXIT key after loading the envelope. All we need, then, is to look at a suitable template for the trickiest of the envelope sizes, C6. Other envelopes are larger, and for the C5 and C4 sizes, you can use the templates for the corresponding paper sizes.

Pick group.
Type name of LAYOUT. STD.
Use **f7,f7,f1** to get to Edit base layout menu.

Left margin at 10, Pitch 10, Line pitch 6, Line space 1.
Right margin 40.

Note: Envelope is to be loaded into printer at extreme left-hand side.

Allow for 3 layout changes, 0 tabs. This allows for layouts for C5, C4 and one other envelope. Allow for two tabs if these are needed for special purposes.

Depth of C5 envelope = 4.4 inches, and with 6 lines per inch, this gives $6 \times 4.4 = 26$ lines altogether. Set for page length of 26 lines, header 0, footer 0. Using zero header will not cause problems, because no footer is being used.

Disable all headers and footers.

Type names and addresses, terminating each with a new page character (ALT RETURN).

Figure 5.6. The template details for a C6 envelope.

Figure 5.6 shows the settings for a C6 envelope template. These numbers are for the loading system described above, in which the envelope is placed at the left-hand side of the printer rather than in the middle. Using a left margin of 10 and right margin of 40 allows up to 30 characters (at 10-pitch) to be used on each line of the address. This should be adequate, and it's better not to use any line longer than this. If any part of an address requires more characters in a line, then the line should be broken into two, as for example:

Polymer Executive &
Professional Services Ltd.

to avoid the unpleasant appearance of one very long line followed by several short ones. The only exception to this rule will occur if the rest of the address needs so many lines that splitting the first one might require you to print too close to the bottom edge of the envelope.
    The template has used 10-pitch, 6 lines per inch, and the normal spacing.

```
        The Office Manager,
        Wordwizz Ltd.
        37 Cranks lane,
        Pondersbury,
        Twits.
```

```
        The Factory Manager,
        Flopsy supplies,
        22 The Burrow,
        Provinder,
        Celts.
```

```
        Mr. G. Urethane,
        Word processor,
        "St. Achter",
        The Street,
        Polymer,
        Suffolk.
```

Figure 5.7. Some sample C6 envelope addressing using the template of Figure 5.6.

For such small envelopes, the use of 12-pitch might be an advantage, but my own feeling, prompted by memories of a postal round as a student, is that an address should be printed in as large a type as possible so that the postman can read it by torchlight on a cold dark December morning. Getting back to layout, no tab stops will normally be needed, and you can allow for three layout changes in the template to cater for the other standard sizes of envelopes. You might possibly require tab stops for particular addressing requirements (such as a bottom line that reads 'Private and Personal'). The number of lines per page is set by using the lines per page × depth formula, giving the page length of 26 lines. The header will be the usual one inch, but we can ignore this and specify zero header and zero footer, since we are unlikely to use either space for the same message on each envelope, unless we need the sender's firm typed on each. The template as shown has disabled headers and footers, because it's better to be able to see what is to be printed on the envelope. If all the text that is to be printed appears in the file, it's easier to visualise the final appearance. If you specify headers and footers, you don't see the effect on the screen, only on the paper. Figure 5.7 shows three envelopes addressed using this template.

At this point, it's important to note some hints and tips on the use of envelope addressing files. To start with, the names and addresses will need to be held in a file for which the envelope template is the base layout. Remember to allow sufficient lines from the start position so that the address starts with its first line about halfway down the envelope. Nine or ten lines is a good setting to try, and for most addresses gives sufficient space for the address lines. The simplest addressing system consists of a list of names which are always used, but things can appear to be less easy if you want to select addresses. Many word processing programs allow for selective printing, so that you can print one address, or a set of consecutive addresses, out of a list. The PCW 8256 system does not permit this, because the whole of a file is recorded on the disc, and all of it is printed. You must not edit your main list, because this would leave the file in the altered state, and you would have to recover the old file from limbo after editing the list. The way around this is to use your template to create a file called TMPFIL which is a temporary file. Each time you want to print a selection from your list of addresses, you edit this file, first copying in the main list, and then editing out the addresses you don't want. The TMPFIL can then be printed on to the envelopes. In this way, the main list is left intact, and only the TMPFIL is altered.

To insert the main file into TEMPFIL, place the cursor over TMPFIL and press E, then ENTER to confirm when the name appears. This puts the PCW 8256 into text edit mode, and loads TMPFIL. Now press f7 and move the cursor down to 'Insert text'. Press ENTER, and you will see the screen change to the Disc managment menu. The message at the top of the screen asks you to pick *destination* drive and group – the message should state *source* drive and group. Position the cursor over your main file of names and addresses in this group, and press ENTER to confirm the choice, then ENTER again when the name of the document appears. The text of the main file will then be loaded into the temporary file, and can be edited as required. See Sections 8 and 9 for details of deleting, moving, copying and exchanging blocks.

One important facility, however, cannot be implemented on LOCO SCRIPT as it stands at the time of writing. Mail-merge means the ability to transfer text from one file to another in a controlled way. For example, you might have a standard letter which has a space for the addressee's name and address, and a 'Dear Someone' start. Using mail-merge, you can keep a list of names and addresses on a separate file and print a set of standard letters, using each name and address in turn. This is the way that magazine publishers can send you a personal letter telling you that you, Jimmy, have probably won a million pounds and you can claim your prize (a plastic covered pocket diary) when you take out a twenty-year subscription. Because of the way the LOCO SCRIPT files are kept on disc, it is likely that a separate mail-merge program can be made available, and such a program will probably be on sale by the time you read this. Another feature of many word processing programs is a spelling checker. The state of spelling is not what it was some thirty years ago, and many people have blind spots either in spelling or in typing. A spelling corrector can compare each word in your document with words in a list, and bring any differences to your attention. This can be a mixed blessing, because it is not always possible to make a checker skip items like names and addresses, though if they are on a separate file the problem doesn't arise. At the time of writing, no spelling checker was available for LOCO SCRIPT, but once again, it will probably be available by the time you read this. Remember that such an action can be very slow, and should be used only where essential.

The next section shows more layouts, one for a business report, one for a business letter, and one for a detailed invoice. All of these are on A4 format, but the settings for the different templates tend to be quite different, and we can make use of items like page numbering on the report. In addition, we shall show how layouts can be changed in the middle of a piece of text, allowing very striking effects – once you get it all right!

Section Six
More Layout Changes

A technical report

In this section, we shall look at some more features of page layout that can be achieved by the use of the PCW 8256 layout menus. Since we have already covered in detail the steps for creating a new template, we don't need to repeat all of these steps here. The first document we shall work with is a technical report, of the type that might be used within an organisation or supplied by a freelance consultant to an organisation. A report of this kind *must* look neat. That does not mean that you must include all kinds of display tricks – contrary to the advice you sometimes get – because this simply makes the report look cluttered. Unless you are trying to cover up ignorance (and a lot of reports do appear to be doing just that), it pays to keep any report brief, accurate, and to the point. Whatever your needs, you will find that the use of the PCW 8256 will fill them except in one useful respect – there is no facility for counting words. For a report, it is more important to count pages, and this is possible. For journalistic work, however, and for authors of articles and books, a word count is very important.

The template details for the report are summed up in Figure 6.1. A centre tab has been put in, but has not been used because in the version of LOCO SCRIPT supplied, the centre tab seemed to be ineffective. Several of the choices, however, need some explanation. To start with, though proportional spacing would produce a better-looking document, the use of 10-pitch character spacing is required if the figures are to be used in a straightforward way. The tab settings have been placed where they might be useful, though they are not necessarily used. As we shall see later in this section, a layout can be changed in the middle of a document, with an entirely different set of tabs, if needed. In the Edit header menu, the slashed zero option has been taken, because the document is imagined to be one produced by an imaginary computer consultant. The **f6** choice is for Widows & orphans prevented. This is the printer's picturesque phrase for single lines from a paragraph which have been left at the end of one page or at the start of the next. By preventing this, we avoid having one line of any paragraph stranded in this way. The other choice is to have paragraphs split (at any point other than the first or last

Key f5 Rename group REPORT.

C (ENTER) Name TEMPLATE.STD.

Key f7 Edit header (ENTER).

Key f7 Options (ENTER).

Key f1 Layout.

Pitch PS, Line pitch 6, Line space 1½, Justify on.

Settings:
Left margin 10, Right margin 70, Clear old tabs.
Ordinary tabs at 15, 20.
Centre tab at 40.
Right tab at 65.
(End of base layout)

Header:
f3 Select slashed zero.
f5 2 layouts, 5 tabs each.
f6 As default (no changes).
f7 PL 70 Head 9 position 6, Foot 7 position 67.
f8 Last page differs.
   First page footer enabled.
   Last page header enabled.
   Last page footer enabled.
(EXIT)

Confirm alterations.

Headers and footers:
Blank for Header 1
Footer 1 is **Page (Centre) (This page No)** == of **(Last Page No)** ≫
Header 2 is **(Centre) W/P Report**
Footer 2 is **(Centre) Last Page-concluded**

Note: Brackets indicate codes as they appear on screen when Codes enabled.

Figure 6.1. The template details for a business report.

line). This is not so objectionable, and this once again is the normal arrangement. You *can* prevent a paragraph from being split if it is absolutely essential to have it all on one page. The page size numbers have been chosen to allow a generous space for header and footer – this is always advisable, because unless the paper is placed very carefully into the printer, it is not easy to ensure consistent footer messages if the footer is right at the bottom of the page. The MANUSCRP template that is provided on your master disc of LOCO SCRIPT places its footer about as low as you can use on a page, and it is not always easy to ensure that the printing of this footer actually lands on the paper.

When the pagination layout option is picked, you are asked to choose how different pages in the document will be laid out. In this case, we want to first page to carry no header, but have a page number at the foot. The last page should carry a header, and a special footer which shows that this is the last page. The intermediate pages should each carry the header, and have a footer of the form – 'Page 2 of 4', using the actual page number and the final page number. We must select the 'Last page differs', with a footer but no header on the first page, and both footer and header on the last page. Once these options have been chosen, the EXIT key brings up the request for confirmation, and this is done by pressing ENTER. You can now put in the copy for the headers and footers, and this requires some care. The header is centred by using the normal **f5** centre choice, and the footer uses the text:

Page (Centre) (this page) == of (last page) >>

to specify text words and numbers. The **this page** and **last page** inserts are *not typed* but obtained from the **f6** menu, and the signs indicate position and number of digits in the page number. The sign == means that the page number will be centred, and will consist of up to two digits. The sign > > means that the number will be to the right of centre and will consist once again of up to two digits. The second header is a copy of the first, and the last page footer carries no page number, only the text 'Last Page – concluded'. Once this last footer has been specified, the EXIT and ENTER keys can be used until the whole layout has been recorded.

Figure 6.2 shows a document which has been produced using this layout. Since the original document was on A4 paper, it cannot be reproduced here full-size, but the use of 10-pitch characters and $1\frac{1}{2}$ line spacing makes it relatively easy to reduce the scale without losing the appearance of the layout. Several points arise here, both as regards the typing of the document, its editing, and subsequent printing. The first point concerns the way that the numbered paragraphs have been inset. This has been done by using a special TAB at the start of the first line of each paragraph. The 'running indent' tab is produced by pressing the ALT key along with the TAB key. The symbol which then shows on the screen is slightly different from the usual tab symbol so that you can see where this has been used on the screen. The effect of this running indent is cancelled by the RETURN key, so that only a paragraph at a time can be indented. You have to remember this, because it's easy to assume that you can place a running indent tab against a sub-title, then obtain a line gap by using RETURN before the next paragraph. The correct procedure is to have the title, if any, normally tabbed, then use the running indent only at the start of a *solid* paragraph of text. On the last page, the

Word Processing.

Assessment of needs

There are three distinct ways in which the use of word processing equipment could materially aid the working of Friendly Consultants Ltd, as presently constituted. In addition, there are likely to be future requirements which will make the use of such equipment necessary, rather than simply desirable. The future computing requirements also make it important to choose a machine which will provide good computing power as well as word processing facilities. In addition, we think that the needs of the Consultancy would be better served by the installation of small machines, using one machine per desk, rather then by using a large computer with several terminals.

The following are the present requirements:

1. The typing of customer reports. Many of these in the past have been of a fairly standardised type, and considerable savings could be made here by keeping a "skeleton" or "template" text into which suitable details could be filled. Even for these reports which are radically different, the use of word processing would save a great deal of time. Several reports in 1982, for example, ran to over 40 pages, and were produced as three draft versions before a final version was approved. All of this represented a considerable waste of time and effort. By using a word processor, several drafts could be made on the screen only, with one printed draft followed by one final version. The

Page 1 of 4

Figure 6.2. A report document produced with the template, prior to editing. The document provides some good arguments for buying the PCW 8256!

W/P Report

only typing effort needed after preparing the first
draft would be the corrections.

2. Maintenance of records. By the nature of the report
work that is carried out, extensive records have to
kept of new developments in the field. These records
are of very different sizes, some only a few lines,
others of more than one page. At present these are
filed in the conventional way, and the filing system is
very awkward to use and maintain. These records would
better be kept as word processing files on discs. It is
possible to record these so that a brief synopsis can
also be recorded and recalled. In this way, finding a
record would be fast and easy, the contents could be
checked without needing to inspect the whole document,
and paper copies could be made as and when needed. It
would be much easier to add to records and amend them
as needed. Security could also be improved for
confidential records, because all the discs that would
be needed could fit easily into a small briefcase and
be taken from the office each evening.

3. Mailing effort could be considerably improved.
During the time of the investigation, one secretary
spent over 72% of the weeks time simply in addressing
envelopes with names of established customers for the
monthly progress reports. This could be avoided by
making the list on the word processor, so that the
envelopes could be addressed using the printer, calling
up the names from a file.

The expansion rate for the business will require
intensive recruitment of new staff if word processing is not
introduced. Since staffing is already a problem in this

Page 2 of 4

Figure 6.2. cont.

W/P Report

area, with more opportunities available than qualified
staff, word processing would, after some initial problems
with training, solve the problem of expanding with existing
numbers. In addition, the elimination of dreary repetition
such as the continual re-typing of draft copies should
considerably improve job satisfaction among existing staff.
It will be important to consult staff fully during the
changeover period, and we strongly recommend that the
partners should familiarise themselves with the fundamentals
of the word processing system before introducing it into the
office. A secretary cannot be expected to learn a new system
by being presented with the machine and its manual. For the
system that we have in mind, there is a book, published
independently, which we can recommend. Using this book,
along with guidance from anyone with experience of the
system will ensure a faster learning rate and will avoid the
frustrations that can arise from trying to find the
appropriate points in the usual type of machine manuals.
    The following are the expected ways in which the
expansion of the business will make the adoption of word
processing essential in the future.

    1. The need for more standardised work such as
    quotations, lists of reference books, modified extracts
    and commentaries.

    2. The likelihood for mail-merge activities, sending
    'personalised' copies for reports to clients rather
    than the 'universal' documents used at present.

    3. The need to use documents in which standardised
    phrases will arise frequently.

Page 3 of 4

Figure 6.2. cont.

W/P Report

CONCLUSIONS

The needs of the office now, and for the immediate future, can be met by installing small low-cost computers with word processing capabilities. Since no computers are used at present, there is no requirement for compatability, and we therefore recommend purchase of the Amstrad PCW 8256 machines. Had the office used any computers with standard-sized discs and a daisywheel printer, the recommendation would have been different. It might well be desirable to attach standard 5¼" disc drives to the Amstrad machines. If this is not done, then we recommend buying the small 3" discs in numbers of not less than 200 so as to ensure a reasonable price. This price will still be three times the cost of a 5¼" disc, but it is important to remember that the small discs are more robust and easier to carry. The cost of the machines is each less than the cost of an electronic typewriter as at present installed.

Jim Stacktop

Hackbit Consultants
June 1986

Last Page - concluded.

Figure 6.2. cont.

heading 'CONCLUSIONS' was the last line of a page in the draft copy. The 'widows and orphans' prevention did not affect this because there is a line space under the word – it is not part of a solid paragraph of text. The problem was solved in this example by inserting another RETURN above the word. There is another method that will be discussed in Section 9. Finally, the $\frac{1}{4}$ character on the last page is obtained by typing ALT-2, using the diagram on page 10 of the PCW 8256 manual.

An invoice

The formal invoice is a very useful candidate for word processing, though most firms will use pre-printed forms for invoices. The advantage of using word processing for invoices is the flexibility that it allows, because the pre-printed form cannot be altered in any way except by scoring out sections that do not apply. For anyone providing a service of a varied nature, rather than supplying goods from a limited list, the use of a word processed invoice can often be an advantage. One important point is that you are not stuck with several thousand identical forms that are no longer useful to you. The form of a word processed invoice can be changed, at each new invoice if necessary, until it suits your needs. Only then need the arrangement be kept. If you like, you can defer putting a template file into the group until the invoice style settles down into something reasonably consistent. This can be very important in the early days of a business, or when things are changing rapidly. Obviously, it takes longer to process an invoice if each pattern is different, but it can take a lot longer to cross bits out of a printed form, and have to staple additional typescript to it!

The template is shown printed out in Figure 6.3. The heading word "INVOICE" is part of the template text, not a header, so that it shows on screen. The firm's name is printed in bold 10-pitch double width italic, making it stand out rather better than normal print. This is then cancelled for the address that follows, returning to 12-pitch. In the template as seen on screen, the columns of name and address reminders that are placed under the words 'SOLD TO' and 'DESPATCH TO' have been put in inverse video. This makes no difference to the printed version, but is a reminder to the user that these parts have to be replaced. The same is true of the items under 'SALES CODE' and 'REMARKS'. All of these replacements are ones that would be made automatically by use of a mail-merging program.

In the next lines, starting with 'DESPATCH DATE', the lettering goes into 15-pitch. This allows more columns of text on the paper, though the effect is not so easy to follow on the screen. The words 'INSERT DATA HERE' are in inverse video on the screen. The 'Unit Price' and 'Amount Due' phrases have had to be positioned with some trial and error so that they correspond to the positions of the decimal tab in the template. Similarly, further down the invoice, the Sub-total, VAT, Carriage & Handling and Total sections are

```
                                INVOICE

WORDANTICS

      Tarboiler House,
      Cyclohex Lane,
      Pollution,
      Staffs.


SOLD TO                         DESPATCH TO

      NAME                            NAME
      ADDRESS                         ADDRESS
      HERE                            HERE
      FIVE                            FIVE
      LINES                           LINES

SALES CODE              REMARKS
HERE                    HERE

DESPATCH DATE    FOB    VIA         ORDER DATE    O/No.    Cat. No.

INSERT DATA HERE

ITEM    QUANTITY   No.    DESCRIPTION                      Unit Price   Amount Due

                              FILL IN THIS















                                                         Sub-total
                                                               VAT
                                                    Carriage & Handling

                                                             Total



           TERMS NET 30 DAYS --- PLEASE PAY THIS AMOUNT
```

Figure 6.3. A printout of a template for a full-sized invoice.

arranged so that money amounts will be positioned by the decimal tab. The footer consists of the message about 30 day terms.

Select group, new document, name TEMPLATE.STD.

Use **f7, f7, f1** to Edit base layout.

Pitch 12, Line pitch 6, Line spacing 1. Italics and justification off.

Left margin 5, right margin 90.

Ordinary tabs at 9, 30, 45, 49.
Decimal tabs at 75, 85.

Note: If the beep sounds and the tab is not positioned, alter the number of permitted tabs from Editing header menu (using **f5**).

Use default page size, header for A4.
Footer zone 7, position 67.

See Figure 6.3 for layout of template.

Figure 6.4. The figures used in setting up the template.

Figure 6.4 shows the form of the template. The most difficult portion lies in the text, in the placing of the 'Unit Price' and 'Amount Due' phrases. The logic behind the positioning is as follows. The decimal tabs have been placed at positions 75 and 85. Now these settings have been measured on the template ruler, which is arranged for 12-pitch text. When 15-pitch is used, position 75 becomes $75 \times {}^{15}\!/_{12}$, equal to 93.75. We have to place the words 'Unit Price', therefore, somewhere around this 93 position and, by trial and error, 92 is found to be suitable. The position 85 for the second decimal tab works out to $85 \times {}^{15}\!/_{12}$ in 15-pitch, giving 106.25, and in this case, 106 turns out to be suitable. Note, however, that these positions are not in line with the decimal tab, either on the screen or on the paper. It rather makes you wonder how the name 'What you see is what you get' ever arose! At least the calculation gives some idea of where to start in the positioning of these items.

Once the template has been adjusted, however, it is there for keeps. It can be tedious having to print out the template and record this new version each time you make a small change, but at least you can use Draft quality for this, and it is a comfort to know that the latest edition is the one that is on the disc. Once the template is secure, you can try out the effect on an invoice with details filled in, as Figure 6.5 illustrates. The example shows that more editing of the template would be useful, particularly in respect of tab positions. In a revised version, we would want layout changes for the DESPATCH DATE lines and the ITEM lines. These changed layouts could then accommodate the

```
                              INVOICE

WORDANTICS

      Tarboiler House,
      Cyclohex Lane,
      Pollution,
      Staffs.


SOLD TO                         DESPATCH TO

      Mr. P.R. Bodger,               Mr. B.F. Trier.
      27 The Prestige,               126 Farthinggale Road,
      LONDON,                        Skellytorn,
      W1                             Norfolk.

SALES CODE            REMARKS
   271/552            Telephone order 24/5/86

DESPATCH DATE    FOB    VIA       ORDER DATE    O/No.     Cat. No.

27/5/86      Flashton  Post        24/5/86      86/M/2167   271/A464

ITEM    QUANTITY  No.    DESCRIPTION                    Unit Price   Amount Due


W/P6        2     B552      W/P outfit  of ribbons,        £27.56     £55.12

                        stationery, cleaners, markers,
                        and discs




                                            Sub-total      £55.12
                                                  VAT      £13.78
                                   Carriage & Handling      £4.70

                                                Total      £73.60



         TERMS NET 30 DAYS --- PLEASE PAY THIS AMOUNT
```

Figure 6.5. An invoice produced with the template in Figure 6.3.

Cursor to Group 3.

Press **f5** (ENTER).
Type BUSLET (ENTER).

Press key **C**.
– Type name TEMPLATE.STD.
– Screen will show some existing template.

Press **f7**, move cursor to 'Editing header', press ENTER.

Screen displays headers/footers. Ignore this.

Press **f7**. Top of screen caption is 'Editing header'.

Press **f1**. Title is 'Editing base layout'.

Use 12-pitch. For this setting of 12 characters per inch, each 10 divisions on printer ruler scale = 12 characters.

For a left margin of 10, use $10 \times 1.2 = 12$.
For a right margin of 70, use $70 \times 1.2 = 84$.

Note: The screen will scroll sideways if needed when you use the left/right-arrow cursor keys.

Press EXIT when settings made, to 'Editing header'.

f3 selects unslashed zero.
f5, f6 remain at default values.
f7 Page size settings:

Page length		70
Header zone		9
position	6	
page body		54
Footer zone		7
position	66	

Note: Header zone of 9 is minimum value. If this is reduced, the footer will be incorrectly placed.

f8 No header first page
Last page differs
Return to page editing by pressing EXIT and ENTER as requested.

f1 Show no codes.

Figure 6.6. A template layout for a business letter of the traditional type.

changes in pitch and new tabs. This would allow the user to fill in the form using tabs rather than the spacebar, and would result in much neater appearance. This is the whole point of using a word processed form – you *can* make such changes. If you had just taken delivery of 5000 printed forms you couldn't do much about it. You can, of course, use your word processed version as a design guide for a printed form, allowing you to make all your mistakes and try your redesigns at a time when it can be done so easily.

A business letter layout

The traditional layout of a business letter is very formal, and is not very widely observed nowadays. Nevertheless, the use of a word processor allows the traditional style to be set up and used very easily, and a group template for such letters on A4 paper is very useful to have. Figure 6.6 illustrates how the template is set up. The default pitch setting of 12 has been used, so that all of the left margin, right margin and tab numbers, which are shown on the printer bail bar for 10-pitch, have been multiplied by 1.2 to get figures applicable for 12-pitch. This gives the figures 12 for the left margin and 84 for the right margin. Remember that the template, once set up, affects each *new* document that is created. The normal default page size values are used, since this is for A4 paper, and the No header option is taken for the first page. The footer is put only on the last page, and consists of the word (End) centred on the line. If the letter consists of one page only, this footer will appear on that page, otherwise on whatever page happens to be the final one.

Figure 6.7 is a letter composed using this template directly, and showing the points that should be observed in a formal business letter of this type. To the template has been added a company name heading, using double width. Obviously, if you were using the template for business use, you would make a suitable heading as part of the template, rather than as part of the letter. In the letter illustration, the title has been created using bold double width 10-pitch, and these settings have been cancelled immediately following the title, so that the remainder of the letter can use the settings of the template. In the template and the letter program, the 'Show' options were to display blanks and effectors only, not codes. This makes sense if you are expecting the screen version to be a reasonably accurate representation of the paper version. When codes are shown, they take up several columns of the display, and make lines which contain them appear to be over-length. On the other hand, it's all too easy if the codes remain invisible, to forget that you are using them. For many letter purposes, however, the main effects are underlining and centring. If only these codes remain invisible, there is little fear of problems arising because the effect of underlining is visible at the time of typing, and the effect of centring becomes visible when the next line is selected.

The important point which starts to emerge here is that the template used when a new document is started is *not* inviolable. In the example above, the

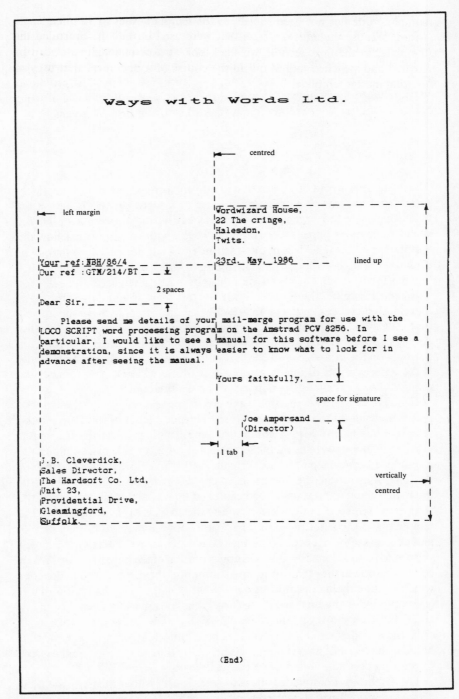

Figure 6.7. A business letter produced using the template, with some reminders of style.

company title has not been subject to the template rules of 12-pitch single width, because the effector codes that were used in this line overruled the template. In the next section, we shall look at how new templates can be created and switched in and out in the course of a document that uses an existing master template.

Section Seven
Template changes

Changing the letter

In the previous section, we looked at how a business letter could be set out, and saw that the template rules could be changed to accommodate a title. In this section, we shall look at how a template can be changed temporarily so as to make use of a completely different template style for part of a document. There is no great difficulty about making the change, but planning the change can be fairly fraught unless you know what effect the change will have. To illustrate this, we shall look at another imaginary business letter, and then at how the layout has been arranged. The letter is shown in Figure 7.1. The base layout is the same as the one used in Figure 6.7, and there is nothing unusual about the first part of the letter. The quotation, however, has used a different layout, with a finer pitch, italic print, justification and different margins. This has been done by designing a new layout immediately after typing the words 'which states:', and then using this layout for the inset paragraphs. At the end of this quote, the original base layout has been restored for the conclusion of the letter. The effect is much more striking than simply insetting the quoted text.

The important point is how all this change is achieved, and Figure 7.2 shows the details. When the base layout itself was created, we allowed for a number of other layouts. If this was not done, then the base layout itself will have to be changed. Assuming that this was done, then when the new layout is needed, the **f2** key is used to bring up the Layout menu. In this menu, the default option that is highlighted when the menu appears is 'brand New layout', and this can be selected by using the [+] key. This brings up the Editing Layout pattern on the screen, but if you look at the title that appears on the top line of the screen, you will see that it refers to Editing Layout **1**. This is the layout number, and once a layout pattern has been created in this document, you will be able to refer to it again if you want to use it at some other place in the *same document*. This implies that details of all alternative layouts are recorded along with your document, and this is why you were advised earlier not to opt for more layouts than you were likely to need, since this will increase the amount of disc space needed and slow down the loading and saving operations.

```
            Keys'n'Fees  Ltd.



                              Unit 7,
                              Logo Ind. Est.,
                              Seeforth,
                              Cambs.

Your ref:AST/22/4            14th. March, 1986
Our ref :BUG/4704/JT

Dear Mr. Tremolo,

    I refer to our recent order for your keyboard synthesiser interface,
model SCREECH/42D. You will no doubt have seen the recent review in
Personal Chip Opinions which states:

        The Tremo-tran model SCREECH/42D has been our least fortunate
        experience so far, Attaching it to any computer has been disasterous,
        and it has blown up three good machines,
              We cannot recommend any reader to buy this device, and we feel
        that you should return any one that you may have bought, On no account
        should it be used, Make sure that you fire insurance is up to date
        even if you only intend to plug it in,

    I am therefore returning this unit under separate cover for your
attention. Please ensure that it is suitably modified, or refund our
remittance of the 24th February.

                        Yours faithfully,



                        Bernie Gigabyte,
                        Quality Controller,
                        Keys'n'Fees Ltd.


Mr. A.S. Tremolo,
Managing Director,
Syntharacket Ltd,
42 Folly Drive,
Sectorville,
Hants.




                            (End)
```

Figure 7.1. A letter, prior to editing, which includes a change of template in the document.

---

1. **f2** Select brand New layout.
2. Use 15-pitch, Line pitch 8, Line space 1, Italic on, Justification on.
3. Left margin 20, right margin 76.
4. Type paragraph that is quotation.
5. Press **f2** and select Base layout.
6. Complete remainder of document.

Figure 7.2. How the layout is changed within the document.

When the Layout menu appears, the choices of 15-pitch, Line pitch 8, Italic and Justification on are selected in the usual ways. The margins and tabs then have to be set. Now this is where you can easily go very far wrong. It's reasonable to suppose that, since you have to multiply all the number settings in the base layout by 1.2 for 12-pitch, you will now have to multipy all the new margin numbers by 1.5 for 15-pitch. You don't, however, *because the number that you use is always determined by the base layout*. In this example, then, the margins are set at around 20 and 76, which represents an indent on each side. The first tab is also left at position 25 – once again, this means a tab in of five 12-point spaces, rather then the smaller 15-point spaces. When you return to editing the letter, the inset paragraph can now be typed. At the end of the quotation, the Layout menu is again selected and this time the cursor is moved to the 'Base layout' legend, and when ENTER is pressed, the layout reverts to the original style.

If you subsequently need the inset layout again, it would not be necessary to recreate it because you now need only get the Layout menu and position the cursor over the Layout ?? space, type in the number of the layout (Layout 1 in this example) and press ENTER. You could also select this Layout 1, edit it and rename it Layout 2 if you wanted to. This ability to create, edit and number any layout is most useful, and the illustrations in the manual for setting tabulated work illustrate how neatly such effects can be achieved. Very little tabulated work has been illustrated in this book because the manual has such good examples.

Identification

When you have several documents in a group, their main identification is by the 'filenames' that you use, like BUSLET.001 and so on. You are often urged to choose names for the documents which reflect what they are, but this is not always so easy, particularly when a group holds a large number of fairly similar documents. If the filename could be made longer, separate identification would be considerably easier, but being confined to eight characters does rather cramp your style. Fortunately, there is another method of identification; the use of the identification menu.

The principle here is that a short piece of text, of up to 90 characters, can be stored on the disc along with your document. This text can be edited like any other text, and it can be replayed separately from the disc. This allows you to keep a short summary of what the main document is about, and to look at this summary alone if you want to know about the document without reading the whole of it. This identity text will appear in a small sub-menu, so that you can still keep an eye on whatever else is on the screen at the time. The identity text is obtained by pressing f2 when the main Menu is on screen.

To create identity text, press the f7 key while the document is on screen. This will bring up the Modes menu, and you should take the cursor down to the 'Identify Text' legend. When you press ENTER on this, you will get a small panel which is headed 'Edit Identify text', and underneath, highlighted, the phrase 'Template for letter group', which you might want to use if what you are identifying is a template, or a letter which contains a template. If you don't want this particular phrase to appear, then it can be deleted by the normal DEL key actions, and you can then type in your own text until the box is filled. The typing is not straightforward, though, because there is no word wrap. In other words, when you come to the right-hand edge of the box, the word that you are typing does not appear on the next line. Instead, the computer beeps at you until you use RETURN to get to the next line. Lines are of up to 30 characters long, and you have to use RETURN to get to the next of the three lines. You can, of course, use the DEL keys to wipe out any part of a word at the end of a line, and then type the whole word on the next line. You can also edit this identifier until it looks just as you want it. When editing is complete, press the ENTER key. The identifier will then be recorded with the rest of the document when you save it. If, of course, you abandon the edit without saving the document, your identifier will not appear.

To get the saved identifier when the Main menu is displayed, position the cursor over the document name and press the f2 = **Inspect** key. The identification text will disappear when you press the ENTER or CAN keys. If there has been no identification text for the document, then what you see depends on what has been in the group. If you are using a new disc with a new template, it's possible that no identification will appear. What is much more likely, however, is that the *wrong* identification will appear! Most of the templates that come with your LOCO SCRIPT disc have had identity texts, and these remain when you edit the templates, unless you create a new identity text. If, for example, you have edited the letters template to produce an invoice, then the identity text will still call any document in this group a 'Template for Letter'! Therefore, if you are going to use the identity text at all, you should create an identity text for each template of your own, and for each document of your own. This at least will avoid confusion.

Section Eight
Copy, Cut and Paste

Up until now, the only editing actions that we have looked at are the deletion of characters by the DEL keys, the insertion of characters by typing them at the appropriate place, and the use of the cursor movement keys to shift position in a document. Even if a word processor contained no more than this editing equipment, it would still be an advance on a typewriter, but the main advantages of using a word processor really start to emerge when you become used to the very flexible advanced editing methods that are open to you. These have deliberately been left until this stage in this book, because if they are introduced too early in the book you tend to be confused by the huge variety of commands whose use you don't really appreciate until you have been using the word processor for some time. If you meet these commands too early, you'll have forgotten what they do when you need them! At this stage, then, when you have established some layouts for yourself and are ready to flex a few muscles, we can look at the editing of a document in more detail.

The first set of commands affect only the movement of the cursor through the document. Before we look at the more involved commands, it's as well to note two variations on the use of the simple cursor keys. If you press SHIFT with a vertical arrowed key, the movement will be 20 lines, up or down. Using SHIFT along with the right or left arrowed keys gives a 40-character movement. If you press ALT with the cursor keys, this will appear to shift the screen text, keeping the cursor in the same place. This applies in *any* direction, so that the screen can be scrolled sideways as well as up or down. This is particularly useful for a layout with a small type size, with perhaps 120 or more characters per line. Since the print on the screen is always the same size, 120 characters can be accommodated only by scrolling the screen sideways, with some of the text always hidden. You should try to avoid using so many characters per line for anything but a short piece of text, however, because it can be very tedious to edit.

The **CHAR** key allows you to move through a text character by character. You might think that this is no more than the right-arrow cursor key does, but there is an important difference. When you use CHAR, spaces are skipped so that the cursor can move from a character at the end of one line to a character midway along the next line if there are only spaces between these characters.

This is a much quicker way of going to characters than the use of the cursor-right or left keys. If you hold down the ALT key along with CHAR (in other words, use ALT CHAR), then the cursor moves backward. This is a general rule; that the use of the ALT key with any of these cursor movement keys will reverse the direction of cursor movement.

WORD is obtained by using SHIFT CHAR, and it moves the cursor from one word to another, putting the cursor on the first character of each word. The movement can appear to be irrational, particularly if text has not been relaid. In particular, you get odd effects at tab stops and at the end of lines. You may find for example, that the cursor moves beyond the last tab stop, or beyond the end of a line, and then goes to the second or third word in the next line, skipping the first word or two. This means that you may have to use ALT WORD (ALT SHIFT CHAR) to move back.

EOL moves the cursor to the end of a line, and will move down one line each time it is pressed, or if held down. Using ALT EOL will move up the lines, with the cursor at the end of each line. The **LINE** action (SHIFT EOL) gives the character at the *start* of each line, moving down for the LINE action, and up if the ALT LINE (ALT SHIFT EOL) set of keys is used. In practice, you would probably find it much easier to use EOL or LINE to get to the correct end of a line, and then use the arrowed cursor keys to move up or down.

PARA allows you to move to the start of the next paragraph, moving down the text as usual if the PARA key is used alone, and up the text if the ALT key is pressed at the same time. When the text contains long paragraphs, it can take a disconcertingly long time to move from one paragraph to the next, and this is one of the less attractive features of LOCO SCRIPT. It becomes even more noticeable using **UNIT** (SHIFT PARA), which moves the cursor to the next marker or to the end of the document (or if used with ALT, to the previous marker or to the beginning). For the use of markers, see the following section. If you have ever used any of the word processing programs in which the shift from the start to the end of a document is almost instantaneous, you will find it very irritating to wait until all the lines of the document have scrolled up or down the screen.

PAGE allows you to move the cursor from a point on one page to the start of the next page, or if ALT is pressed, to the start of the previous page. Once again, this is a slow change, because all the lines are displayed on the way. Using SHIFT PAGE gives **DOC**, which provides the end of the document or, using ALT, the start, and is another slow action identical to that of UNIT when no markers are used.

Block movements

One very important feature of word processing editing which we haven't looked at so far is block editing. A block is a section of continuous text which

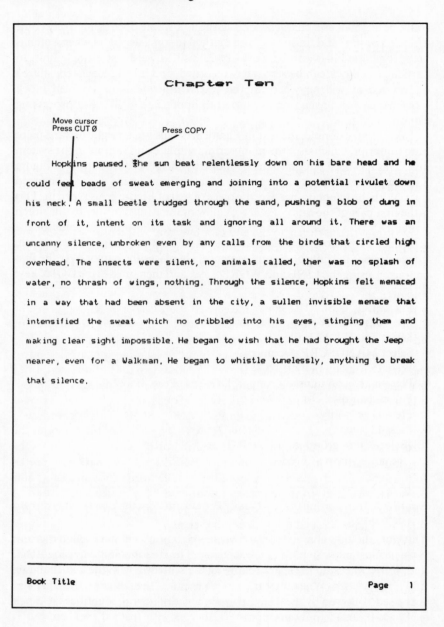

Figure 8.1. A sample of manuscript on which cut and paste editing can be used. The cursor position at which the COPY key is pressed has been shown.

could be as small as a character or as large as a whole document. To become a block, the start and finish has to be marked in some way, and when that has been done, the block can be worked with as if it were just a single unit. In particular, a block can be separately recorded, and it can be deleted, shifted or inserted at will anywhere in the text. Until you have sampled block movements, you haven't really started to appreciate what word processing can do for you.

Take, as an example, the text in Figure 8.1. This is a straightforward piece of manuscript, which uses the manuscript template and sample in the system disc. This has been put on to the data disc by the procedure shown in Figure 8.2, using Drive M as a temporary store for the file when the discs are changed over. With the template in place, the piece of text of Figure 8.1 is typed in. This is the first part of the draft of a new 'Valley of the Kings' thriller by the noted writer D.S. Lexya and, as usual, he doesn't like the order of some of the sentences. How does he make alterations without retyping? To start with, Lexya decides to shift the second sentence. He places the cursor over the first character, using the LINE and WORD keys, and then presses the COPY key.

1. Put in LOCO SCRIPT copy.
2. Press **f1** to notify change (log in disc).
3. Select TEMPLATE file.
4. Select MANUSCRP document.
5. Press **f5** to copy file.
6. Place cursor on unused group in Drive M. Press ENTER.
7. Put in data disc.
8. Press **f1** to notify.
9. Press **f3** to copy.
10. Select spare group in disc A/B. Press ENTER.
11. Rename group as needed.

Figure 8.2. Transferring the MANUSCRP template from the Start-of-day disc on to a data disc.

This puts the first character into inverse video, showing dark against green. Now he must mark the end of the sentence. The cursor is shifted, using LINE and WORD keys, to the space following the sentence, with the text changing into reverse video. When the cursor is at the end of the sentence, the CUT key is pressed, followed by the 0 key. This sequence of actions identifies the block as Block 0, and it now disappears (rather slowly) from the screen, but is retained in the memory.

To check blocks, press **f8**. This will show the numbers of any marked blocks, and allow you to save a block separately on disc, in case you want to insert it into another piece of text. If you only want to check that the block is present, press CAN to cancel any action.

Now the author can relay the text. It now looks as in Figure 8.3. Having the

<pre>
                        Chapter Ten

        Hopkins paused. A small beetle trudged through the sand, pushing a blob
   of dung in front of it, intent on its task and ignoring all around it. There
   was an uncanny silence, unbroken even by any calls from the birds that circled
   high overhead. The insects were silent, no animals called, ther was no splash
   of water, no thrash of wings, nothing.░Through the silence, Hopkins felt
   menaced in a way that had been absent in the city, a sullen invisible menace
   that intensified the sweat which no dribbled into his eyes, stinging them and
   making clear sight impossible. He began to wish that he had brought the Jeep
   nearer, even for a Walkman. He began to whistle tunelessly, anything to break
   that silence.
</pre>

Book Title   Page 1

Figure 8.3. The text of Figure 8.1 after cutting the marked section.

dung-beetle right at the beginning is less menacing, allowing a slower build up of tension. Now he can add a few words to that sentence, and put in the text about the sun beating down.

To insert a block, put the cursor at the point where the text is to be inserted. This is going to be immediately before the sentence that starts 'Though the silence..'. With the cursor in place, press PASTE and then type 0. This means that the text of Block 0 is to be put into this point in the document. The block numbering system allows ten blocks to be marked and manipulated in this way, using identification numbers of 0 to 9. Note that this method deletes a block and pastes it in elsewhere. If you need to *copy* a block, leaving the original intact, then substitute COPY 0 for CUT 0 at the end of the block. If you do this, the text reverts to normal video, and remains in place, but can be pasted wherever else you want it. This can be a very useful technique if you have to put in several copies of a piece of text.

Now the text looks as in Figure 8.4, with the beads of sweat section in its new position. All of these steps would, of course, have been done on screen rather than on paper as we see them here, and only the final version would be printed. Before this is done, Lexya would presumably have noticed the missing 'e' at the end of 'there', following 'no animals called' and the misspelled 'now' in the 'sweat in the eyes' sentence, and corrected these. Figure 8.5 then shows the final version, in High quality print style. Oddly enough, authors seem to commit more mistakes of this kind when using a word processor than they did before word processors became available. Some believe that this is because a secretary would have typed the work in days gone by, but a contributory factor is the difficulty of working on screen. It is an undisputed fact that it's more difficult to spot mistakes on a screen than on a piece of paper. I don't know why this should be so, but it is. You should therefore look more carefully at text on the screen, and if the work is important and not too long, you should print a draft copy and proofread that. This applies particularly to important letters (job applications, CVs, etc.), and rather less to book manuscripts, which will in any case be checked by eagle-eyed editors. Articles for magazines should be proofed very carefully because if deadlines are involved, mistakes may not be picked up at the editing stage.

Now if this piece of shifted text had been recorded on a disc, it could have been inserted into place from disc, rather than from block memory. In addition, it could have been put into a different manuscript, even one that was held on a different disc.

To save a block on disc, mark it with COPY and CUT (number) as before, then call the Block menu by pressing **f8**. Place the cursor on 'Save block ??' and type the number of the block. Press ENTER, and you will be presented with the Main menu, with a message at the top of the screen which asks you to pick a destination group and drive. If you want to save on the disc that you are presently using, pick Drive A (or B if this is your drive), any suitable group (preferably one with the same template), and then press ENTER. Picking in this sense means moving the cursor over the group and drive legends. *If you*

Chapter Ten

Hopkins paused. A small beetle trudged through the hot pale sand, pushing a blob of dung in front of it, intent on its task and ignoring all around it. There was an uncanny silence, unbroken even by calls from the birds that circled high overhead. The insects were silent, no animals called, ther was no splash of water, no thrash of wings, nothing. The sun beat relentlessly down on his bare head and he could feel beads of sweat emerging and joining into a potential rivulet down his neck. Through the silence, Hopkins felt menaced in a way that had been absent in the city, a sullen invisible menace that intensified the sweat which no dribbled into his eyes, stinging them and making clear sight impossible. He began to wish that he had brought the Jeep nearer, even for a Walkman. He began to whistle tunelessly, anything to break that silence.

Book Title   Page   1

Figure 8.4. The copied block of text pasted into its new position.

Chapter Ten

Hopkins paused apprehensively. A small scarab beetle trudged through the hot pale sand, pushing a blob of dung in front of it, intent on its task and ignoring all around it. There was an uncanny silence, unbroken even by calls from a vulture that circled high overhead. The insects were silent, no animals called, there was no splash of water, no thrash of wings, nothing. The sun beat relentlessly down on his bare head and he could feel beads of sweat seeping from his scalp and joining into a saline rivulet down his neck. Through the silence, Hopkins felt menaced in a way that had been absent in the city, a sullen invisible menace that intensified the sweat which now dribbled into his eyes, stinging them and making clear sight impossible. He began to wish that he had brought the Jeep with its radio nearer, even the sound of his Walkman. He began to whistle tunelessly, anything to break that silence.

Doom in the Desert   Page   1

Figure 8.5. The final version of the section of manuscript, printed with high quality print.

want to save the block on another disc, place the cursor over a group in Drive M and press ENTER. Then save your manuscript (using EXIT) on the present disc, change discs, notify the change with **f1** and copy (from the block file from Drive M) to a group in the new disc.

To insert a block from a disc into your current text, you must have the block either on the current disc or in Drive M. If you do not have the block on the same disc, you have to put your text on disc, change discs, get the block of text into Drive M, then change back to the disc which contains the main text. With the main text in place, you press **f7** to get the Modes menu, and use the cursor keys to select Insert text. When you press ENTER, you will get the Main menu, and a reminder on the top of the screen. This message is misleading, because it asks you to pick a *destination* group and drive. What you are picking, of course, is a *source* group and drive. When you pick the group and drive (A, B, or M) using the cursor, and press ENTER, the text is moved. If Drive M has been used, the transfer is almost instantaneous, but if a disc drive is used, you will see the text being moved on the screen.

Text can be removed completely by much the same process, but pressing the CUT key at each end of the block, rather then the COPY key. Both of these actions will work 'in reverse', meaning that if, for example, you press the COPY key at the end of a block, and put the cursor back to the start of the block to press CUT 0, the block will be saved in the same way. Using PASTE 0 on this block will put the block back into the text in the correct order, not reversed. This allows a little more flexibility in the operation if you happen to be going through the text in reverse order.

These cut, copy and paste techniques are even more useful in letters and standard documents than on manuscripts. You can, for example, record a standard letter and a list of names and addresses on a disc. You can then make a copy of this file and edit it, with a name and address pasted into the correct place and the other names and addresses deleted. Printing this file will give a letter to one particular addressee, and the process can be repeated as often as you like. An improvement is to keep the standard letter and the name/address list as two separate files, and insert both into a temporary file when needed. This removes the risk of saving a mutilated file of the standard letter or name list. Unfortunately, LOCO SCRIPT makes no provision for 'locking' any file so that it can't be written over and replaced by editing, so you have to be careful about this. For such insertion methods, it's often better to work with the files in Drive M, so that the files on the disc are always protected. My own preference is to keep all important files of this kind on a disc which is write-protected, so that nothing can be written back on to the disc. This forces me to use Drive M and ensures security of files. If it took you several weeks to type all the data into one disc set of files, you'll want to ensure that it remains safe.

Section Nine
Other Editing Actions

Boilerplating

Boilerplating is not a word that you'll find in the PCW 8256 manual, but it is the term used in word processing to describe the use of stock phrases. Just as a boiler can be made up from steel panels that are pre-shaped and need only be welded together, so many letters of a particular type can be built up from stock phrases. The method of adding text from a disc that we looked at in the preceding section is one way of boilerplating, but the PCW 8256 offers another method of building up text with standard phrases. These phrases are particularly useful for business letters, but they are also of great interest for journalists and book authors. The principle is that a set of standard phrases can be held in memory – the LOCO SCRIPT system disc contains a few phrases that are useful for estate agents, for example. These phrases can be created and edited, and they are particularly easy to insert in a document. These phrases should be held on the LOCO SCRIPT system copy disc rather than on a data disc. The point about using the LOCO SCRIPT copy is that this is your Start-of-day disc, the one from which LOCO SCRIPT is loaded. The action of loading in LOCO SCRIPT also loads the memory (Drive M) with the standard phrases. If you keep standard phrases of any kind separately on a data disc, you will have to load them into Drive M separately, which is yet another operation. In this section, we'll look at these options in detail.

To start with, the system disc of LOCO SCRIPT that comes with your PCW 8256 contains a set of standard phrases for estate agents, and these will be on your copy also. To see what standard phrases are available, select a spare document file and load it. Wipe out the contents using the CUT key, and then press the f8 key. In the section labelled 'Phrase', you will see the letters ABCD KM PRS Z. Each of these letters represents a standard phrase. Any one phrase can be up to 255 characters, but the total number of characters in all the phrases must not exceed about 550 characters. Because one letter of the alphabet is used to identify each phrase, you can have up to 26 phrases providing the total character count does not exceed the maximum of 550, and that no phrase is longer than 255 characters.

Figure 9.1 shows the standard phrases on your LOCO SCRIPT disc copy. These have been obtained by using PASTE, followed by the *letter* of each phrase, and the result has been edited to put in the phrase letters also. Note that letters are used to paste in phrases, numbers to paste in blocks of text from the same document. Unless you happen to be an estate agent you will probably not want this particular set of phrases, and if they are useful to you, you will probably want to add more. The method of creating phrases and putting them on to the Start-of-day disc, then, is of considerable importance.

To start with, keep your ordinary data file disc in place. Do not start to change anything on your Start-of-day disc until you are sure that the phrases you have in stock are the ones you will want. Select a template which allows you plenty space, like the manuscript one. Now type all of the phrases that you might want to use. It's at times like this that you wish LOCO SCRIPT had a character or word count, because it would make the preparation of this text a lot easier. As it is, you just have to hope that by keeping the phrases short you will be able to stay within the limit. As the manual advises, it's a good idea to start by making sure that you delete the old **Z** choice, since this uses up a large part of the available character allocation. To get rid of an old phrase, you have to record a new one with the same letter. If, for example, you put the cursor over a blank line in your document and then press COPY, followed by CUT Z, you will have deleted phrase Z from the entry.

Once you have your list of phrases, you can edit it until all mistakes have been removed, and you can store it on disc under a different heading, just in case you want to alter it. The reason for this will become obvious later. You can then return to your file of phrases and record them as phrases. For each phrase, place the cursor at the start of the phrase and press the COPY key. Move the cursor to the end of the phrase and press the CUT key (or COPY again), followed by the letter that you want to use to identify the phrase. This records the phrases in memory. You can then make a recording of all the phrases on the disc. This is done by pressing key **f8** and putting the cursor over the Save all phrases legend. Pressing ENTER will then save the phrases as a special file, PHRASES.STD, which will be put into Group 1, Drive M when the disc is a Start-of-day disc.

If you now want to put these phrases on to your Start-of-day disc, then place this disc in the drive and press **f1** to notify the change. Now copy the PHRASES.STD file from Group 0, Drive M into Group 0, Drive A. This is done by erasing the existing file of PHRASES.STD (key **f6**) on the Start-of-day disc, then placing the cursor over the PHRASES.STD file in Drive M, pressing **f4**, ENTER, then placing the cursor over any file in Group 0, Drive A and pressing ENTER again. Once all this has been done, your Start-of-day disc contains your new phrases. It all looks rather complicated, but it's better than working all the time with the rather valuable Start-of-day disc. You still have your phrases as a separate file on another disc, and you can use this for editing or similar purposes.

```
A    double aspect
B    on frequent bus route
C    convenient for the M62
D    deceptively spacious
K    kitchen/breakfast room
M    in need of some modernisation
P    panelled bath
R    reception rooms
S    ideally situated

Z    The computer is called the PCW8256 and it runs LocoScript, which is
simple to use.    This is my first letter.    It only tookk me about twenty
minutes to get it free of spelling and laid out the the way I wanted.
```

Figure 9.1. The standard phrases on the Start-of-day disc, showing the letter that corresponds to each phrase.

Figure 9.2 shows a set of phrases which have been created as a separate file and then saved as PHRASES.STD on the Start-of-day disc. You can, of course, still follow the alternative path of storing these phrases on a separate disc and transferring them into the memory, Drive M, Group 0, after you have switched on. Don't think that the method involving the Start-of-day disc is the only one open to you; it just happens to be the most convenient for many purposes. If it happens that you want to keep several sets of phrases for different purposes, then there's nothing to stop you having several sets on each data disc, and loading them into Drive M Group 0 as and when you want to use them. Figure 9.3 shows a piece of work which has been turned out using the phrases in Figure 9.2. You can see that the phrases have been used extensively, so that very little typing has been needed for the whole piece. There is scope here for even more phrases to be used (and correction to be made!). In many applications, of which estate agency, car sales and domestic appliances represent three good examples, advertisements and letters can often consist almost exclusively of boilerplated phrases of this type, so that such work can be created very quickly. If a suitable template is made, then camera-ready copy can be generated, saving considerably on printing costs.

Providing you do not exceed the character limits, your phrases need not be single lines. You can, for example, store a name and address, complete with tabs and carriage returns, as a phrase. Since an name and address contains, on average, between 80 and 100 characters, you should get at least five of them into a PHRASES.STD file. For small groups of names and addresses, this offers an interesting alternative way of getting such items into your text. Note, however, that you can only paste into text. You cannot use the PASTE key when you are asked for a phrase as a filename, for example, or in any application where you have to type a name into a sub-menu. This is particularly unfortunate when it comes to using the EXCH key, as we shall see in the next section.

```
Excellent finish
50 mpg at 56 mph
Power steering
Electric windows
Central locking
Large boot
Hatchback
Adjustable steering wheel
Range of engine sizes
Optional automatic transmission
Heated rear window
Passenger door mirror
No rust
Good little runner
Remarkable for its year
```

Figure 9.2. A new set of phrases, saved on the MANUSCRP template before being transferred to the PHRASES.STD file.

```
                    NBG 218 GTI

This  is  a  good  little  runner,  our  managing  Directors
personal  transport.  Features  power  steering,  electric
windows,  central  locking,  adjustable  steering  wheel  and
passenger  door  mirror.  Remarkable  for  its  year,  no  rust.
Only £9395. Two weeks warranty.
```

Figure 9.3. A document, prior to editing, that makes use of the new phrases.

Section Ten
More Block Actions

Using UNIT

In Section 8, we saw that the use of the UNIT key on a piece of text had the same effect as the use of the DOC key. This, however, was only because the document that was in use had no markers inserted. To get some experience with this, select the group with the manuscript template, and create a new document. You can remove the existing parts of the templated material by using CUT, and then fill in with material from another document. This is done by selecting the Modes menu (f7) and bringing the cursor down to Insert text, then pressing ENTER. You are then shown the Main menu and asked to pick a suitable group and drive. Once again, the text on the top of the screen contains the phrase 'destination', but means 'source'. When you press ENTER the title appears, and a second press of ENTER confirms that this is the document you want. The document will now be inserted into the template. This method allows you to create a new filename document which is identical to an old document. If you use the Edit command, you will replace the document whose name you use, and this is not always desirable, particularly when you want to experiment with a document.

With the text in place, choose a word somewhere near the end of the text, and position the cursor over the first character.

To mark a character, use the UniT selection in the SET menu. You can do this by calling up the SET menu (press [+] and the chequered key) and placing the cursor over UniT, then pressing [+], or simply by pressing [+]UT in succession. You will see the text split on the screen when you do this, because of the insertion of invisible marker codes. If you make the codes visible by taking the Codes option in the f1 menu, you will see that the word (UniT) has been inserted. You can now move the cursor to the top of the document by using the DOC key. Now that a unit marker has been inserted, the UNIT key will find this place rather than the end of the document. You can put in more than one UniT, and pressing the UNIT key will then take you from one marker to the next. There is, in theory, no limit to the number of markers you can insert, but the alternative methods of finding material, such as the PARA key, make it unnecessary to have a large number of UniT markers.

To find the marked position, from the top of the document, press the UNIT key. If you are working from the bottom of the document, you need to use the ALT UNIT keys (ALT SHIFT PARA keys). If you have several markers inserted, the UNIT key will take you to the next marker down the document; and ALT UNIT will take you to the previous marker. As usual, the movement is slow because each line has to be shown on the screen, and you will often find that lines have to be relaid on the way. Note that the UniT is only a single marker – it is not normally put at both the start and the end of a section. You could, however, mark the start and the end of a section that you might later want to move or delete, because the use of the markers would make the section easy to find. Unfortunately, the markers have to be deleted individually when you want to remove them; there is at present no provision for deleting all of the markers in a text with one command, since the EXCH key (see later in this section) will not accept the UNIT key as one of its 'phrases'. On the other hand, you don't really need to remove markers unless you have so many that the use of the UNIT key becomes cumbersome.

The main use for the UniT marker is to enable you to find something that would not otherwise be obvious. You wouldn't, for example, use it to mark the start of a paragraph or indented material, because these can be found by other methods. Obviously, you need to know at the time you type the material that there will be something you will want to find easily in this way. A novelist, for example, might want to mark each point where the name of a character was mentioned. In legal documents, you might want to find each reference to case law quickly; in an engineering report, you might want to mark each word that was an engineering term. Another possibility for authors is the marking of each word that should appear in an index. At the time of writing, no automatic indexing program is available for use with LOCO SCRIPT, but the use of UniT, together with the fact that the pages are numbered, makes the writing of such a program relatively simple for a programmer. The important point about UniT is that the markers remain along with the text, whether you make them visible or not. When a piece of recorded text is edited, then, you can still find its embedded markers and use them to find out what words were marked in this way. One particularly helpful use is to mark sections in a template which will have to be removed when the template is used. Examples are the 'ADDRESS HERE' and 'NAME HERE' in letter templates. By marking these points, it's easy to locate them for use with CUT.

Search and replace

Two actions that are essential to word processing are the search and replace facilities. These allow you to find a particular word or phrase in a piece of text, and to shift the cursor there. Alternatively, you can find a word or phrase and replace it with another word or phrase. If the word or phrase occurs several times in the text, you can choose global search and replace, which means that each occurrence of the word/phrase will be found and the replacement carried out. An alternative is selective replacement, in which each find action causes a pause until you signal that you want the replacement carried out or not. As usual, the yea or nay action is carried out using the [+] and [−] keys.

To see this in action, first of all remove all the markers you may have put in. This has to be done marker by marker, remember; there is no provision for removing all the markers with one keypress. The easiest way is to use the UNIT key to go to a marker, and then tap the left-delete key once to remove the marker. Now go to the top of the document, using the word processing report document as an example which is long enough to show the methods in action. We can now search for the word 'customer'.

To find a word, press the FIND key. A sub-menu will appear, inviting you to type in the word that you are looking for. Type the word **customer**, and then press ENTER. You will see the text scrolling until the cursor is over the first letter of the first appearance of this word. The text scrolling will be slow, particularly if text is being relaid on the way because of the removal of markers.

To find the next occurrence of the same word, press FIND again, and when the menu appears press ENTER, since the original word will still be in place. If the word does not occur again, the cursor will be left at the end of the document.

When you want to find a phrase, you need to remember that the phrase must fit into the box that appears when you press the FIND key. This box will hold up to 30 characters, and you must be certain that you will delete any characters of a word or phrase that you formerly used. Each space is indicated in the box by a dot to help you to lay out your phrase. The phrase that you type must be absolutely identical to any phrase that you are looking for, particularly as regards capital letters, spaces, and any carriage returns. You do *not*, however, need to include items like underlining, bold type or other 'effectors'.

The finding action can be a useful alternative to using a UniT marker, mainly because FIND does not require any action in advance. On the other hand, FIND does not leave any marker at the found position, so you can combine the two by using FIND to locate key words, and then leaving a marker at each one by use of UniT. Note that FIND works in one direction only, from the cursor position in a document downwards. You cannot use ALT FIND to find words by moving up a document.

The FIND action can be useful in placing effectors, or in cut and paste operations. For example, you can place the cursor over the first character in a set that you want underlined, and press the usual [+]W keys. You can then use the FIND key to 'find' the word at the end of the section that you want underlined. Pressing ENTER on this will cause the underlining to take place along the whole section, and you can then shift the cursor to the end of the last word and press [–]UL to terminate the underlining. You can similarly place the cursor, press the CUT key, and then use FIND to get to the end of the section that you want to cut, pressing the CUT key again at that point. You can similarly use the FIND key facility with COPY and PASTE. Used wisely, and with some practice, these facilities can be a very considerable help in making the best of a document.

Exchange

Exchanging is an action that needs to be carried out with more care. When words are exchanged, the machine does so blindly, and it's possible to make exchanges which will have ridiculous results. For example, if you exchange each smith for jones, you may find a word blackjones which is new to you, and to the Collins Dictionary! This has to be watched, in particular, when correcting spelling or typing mistakes with an EXCH key command. Suppose, for example, that you have a bad habit of typing 'will' as 'wil'. You could exchange each wil for will in a document – and then find that each will has become 'willl' as a result. The correct method of avoiding this is to exchange each wil(space) for will(space), putting in the spaces deliberately so that the program looks for the space as well as for the letters. Since 'will' does not have a space following the first 'l', the incorrect exchange cannot happen.

To make an exchange, move to the appropriate place in the document, usually the top. Press the EXCH key (SHIFT FIND), and you will see the Exchange menu appear. The highlighted part indicates where you can type the word or phrase that is to be found. Remove any word that is here, using the DEL keys, and type **business**. Now use the down-cursor key to get into the replacement box. In this box type **dental practice**. Now shift the cursor down to the line that reads 'Automatic exchange to end of Doc.', and press ENTER. Your replacement of 'business' by 'dental practice' will then proceed throughout the document. As usual, this will be slow because the phrase that is being used for replacement is not of the same size as the original, so relaying of text has to be done. This is a feature of WYSIWYG (what you see is what you get) word processing, and for really fast text manipulation, you really have to use a word processor of the 'post-formatted' type, like Wordwise Plus on the BBC Micro.

The Exchange menu offers you several other choices. You can, for example, choose to carry out replacement only from the present cursor position to the end of a paragraph, or to the end of a page. You can also opt to confirm each exchange. If you take this option, which is the default option, then each time the target word or phrase is found the cursor will pause on it, waiting for you to signal replace (press [+]) or not replace (press [–]). As with FIND, the set up of word/phrase in the Exchange menu remains until you substitute something else. You also have the same limitations as in the FIND action that you cannot put a phrase into the Exchange lines from your stock phrases, or from a file.

The search and replace facilities are extremely useful for actions which would be tedious if you had to type each change. Unfortunately, you can't incorporate items like underlining into the replacement text. It would be very useful if, for example, you could replace each occurrence of 'typing' by 'typing', but this is not possible, nor can you replace underlining by bold type, just to name one example. The main use, then, is to allow a fairly standard letter to be used for several purposes, as the example has indicated. Another very common use is to avoid typing certain words. In a book, I might have to type the word 'microprocessor' several hundred times. By abbreviating this to M/, something that would not occur normally in text, I can use a search and replace action to replace each M/ by microprocessor. This should not be done to excess, otherwise there is a risk that you will lose track of your abbreviations, unless you keep them as standard phrases, with a key to the letters written where you can see it easily as you type. One considerable advantage of using search and replace is consistency. If you replace each M/ by microprocessor, you need spell 'microprocessor' correctly only the one time. This avoids typing errors that can occur when constantly typing the same word over and over again.

One warning is needed here, particularly for book authors. The use of FIND and EXCH is something that tempts you to work with large pieces of text, so that all the work can be done in one effort. You will normally work in chapters, but it's better still to work in shorter sections, perhaps half or even quarter chapters. This allows you to work with shorter documents. This is a considerable advantage with LOCO SCRIPT, particularly if you need to search around a document a lot. As we have seen, this action is very slow, and the longer the document the slower it becomes. When you rework a document, it's a good idea to create a new document with a new title (CHAP6C.003 for example) for each revision. This is because if you use the Edit command, you will be replacing the previous version each time. The previous version then becomes a 'limbo' file, which can be recovered, but the version before that is gone for ever. We'll see later, in Section 13, how limbo files can be recovered, but if you like to rework your text a lot it's as well to use different filenames each time. For example, when you create CHAP6B.003, you can start by inserting the text from CHAP6B.002 or from CHAP6B.001 as you choose, depending on how you want to rework the text. When each chapter section has reached its final version, you can join the sections by placing all the sections in order into a new file. This will be the final section file, and you can then carry out any finishing touches (exchange 'desert' for 'rolling waves') on this one. Of course, you might like to follow the example of Oscar Wilde who, asked what he had done that morning, said that he had put in a comma. When asked what he would do in the afternoon he said: 'Take it out again'.

Section Eleven
Niceties of Layout

Rulers, blanks and spaces

This section is concerned with odds and ends of topics that affect the way you see the document or the way in which it is printed. The first point concerns the options in the Show menu, selected with **f1**. The default here is to display codes, such as the SET menu words, where these are used in the text. Displaying codes is very useful when you want to see where these have been inserted, but when the codes are displayed, the text on the screen is not an exact representation of what you see on the paper. You don't for example, print the words (+Wordul)CONCLUSIONS(−UL), only the word <u>CON-CLUSIONS</u>, so that the appearance on the screen is deceptive. This is particularly true if you are going to print text justified. The best method of dealing with this is to have the codes displayed as you type the document, but remove them when you want to check it just before printing. This is the normal action on the 'post-formatted' type of word processor. If the text is stored on the disc with codes removed, it's a good idea to display the codes again if you are going to edit the text, so that you can see what you are removing or adding to. You should keep codes displayed when you are using things like name headings in 10-pitch double width bold italic, because none of this shows on screen unless you show codes. On the other hand, if you want to see how tabulated work looks when you are using codes for things like italics and bold type, then you need to use codes to check that they are in the correct places, and then remove the on screen codes so that you can check the tabulation. Once again, what you see is not necessarily exactly what you get!

Blanks and spaces are also offered in the State of menu. If you opt to show blanks, the screen will display a dot for each character position not occupied by a character. This can be a useful guide to positioning text, and is used in most of the standard templates. If you opt to show spaces as well, each space, meaning each place at which you pressed the spacebar, will be marked with a large bullet-shaped dot. This can also be a useful guide, but to my eyes at least it's not something that I want to have on screen for very long. For working on long documents, like articles and book chapters, it's better, in my mind to have both the spaces and blanks switched off so that the eye can concentrate on text. On the other hand, if you are laying out tabular work in which positioning of characters is very important, then you can find the display of blanks and spaces a definite advantage. Display of blanks and spaces is useful when justified text is being typed, because it shows better how the text will be arranged in the line.

Display of rulers applies only when you make several changes of template in a document. The ruler is the line at the top of the screen which shows the column numbering with margin and tab positions. By taking the Rulers option in the State of menu, you will produce a ruler line in the text at each point where a layout change has occurred. If you turn to the business letter to Mr Tremolo (Figure 7.1), you will see the effect of choosing the Rulers option. Once again, the display of rulers is of particular use when the text is being typed originally, or when it is being reworked extensively. Displaying the rulers in the text can save some eye movement, but remember that you have the other option of placing the cursor on the top line where the normal ruler is in any case, and moving the text lines up or down to the cursor.

Soft and hard breaks

One problem that affects a lot of printed work is how a line breaks. Suppose, for example, that you have in your text the item 'Price £ 20', with a space between the pound sign and the '2'. You would not like this to be printed so that the pound sign appeared at the end of one line and the figure 20 on the next. Obviously you would avoid this when you typed the text, but if the text is to be printed justified, then the split may occur when the text is relaid. To avoid this, we can put in what is called a 'hard space' between the parts of a phrase. The alternative here is not to have a space in the phrase at all, but this is not always an option that you can take.

To insert a hard space, we type the first part, in this example the £ sign, then use the **f5** key, and move the cursor to 'insert hard space' and press ENTER. This inserts the hard space, which appears on the screen (if enabled) as a curled dash, then the figure can be typed. Now, no matter how this piece of text is moved about the screen, it will never be split. The alternative method of inserting the hard space, which is easier, is to press the [+] key and then the spacebar. Note that the hard space will appear as a code on screen only if spaces have been enabled by the **f1** menu. If space markers have not been enabled, the hard space appears as any other space in a document.

The soft space does not normally show on screen as a space, nor unless enabled as a code, nor does it print out. Where it *does* appear is when a break occurs across two lines, leaving the word before the soft space at the end of one line, and the word following on the next line. For example, if you type the word type([-]space)script, in which the item in brackets represents the insertion of a soft space by using the [-] key followed by the spacebar, then this word appears on screen as the word 'typescript', and will print in this fashion. If, however, the word is moved about and the text relaid so that the word reaches the end of a line, another insertion into the line will cause the word 'type' to appear at the end of one line, with 'script' at the start of the next. There will be no spaces between the sections. The general rule, then, is that a hard space shows as a space but does not allow a word to be split, and a soft space does not show normally, but does allow a word to be split at the soft space position. When spaces are shown on screen, the soft space appears as a hard-space character within brackets.

The hard and soft hyphens behave in similar ways. If you hyphenate a word with a hard hyphen, you will never get the word split at the hyphen. The hard hyphen is obtained using the [+] key and hyphen key. You would use this when you have a hyphenated word like Start-of-day which you didn't want to be split. The soft hyphen (which shows on the screen as a hyphen in brackets) is obtained by using [–] and hyphen, or by use of the Lines menu. One point you should be careful about is that if you relay text so that a word splits with a soft hyphen, then any attempt to rejoin the word can sometimes cause trouble. If you delete words from the upper line, then attempt to relay the text, you will often find that a few squiggly line symbols appear, and the keyboard locks up entirely. Your only option then is to switch off, because pressing the restart keys (EXIT SHIFT EXTRA) will not normally restore control. You will have lost any text not saved on disc, which is yet another argument for saving text at frequent intervals, by taking the 'Save and Continue' option when you press EXIT on a text.

Determining page boundaries

The use of hard and soft spaces and hyphens is a useful way of controlling how text is split, or not split, at the end of a line. It may be equally important to determine what happens at the start or end of a page. Taking the example of the fictitious word processing report again, the heading CONCLUSIONS was on a line which should not have appeared at the end of a page, with its following text on the next page. At the time, we avoided the split simply by putting in an extra carriage return. Another way to avoid the split, however, is to indicate that the previous page must end immediately above this word. This is done by typing [+]LL, or by using the Pages menu (on **f6**) and the cursor to put in the Last Line code. This applies if you can see on the screen that the heading is going to come at a page boundary. If, however, you intend to change templates on this text later, and you want to ensure no page break at the time of printing, you can take the cursor to the line that contains the heading and type [+]k3 (ENTER). This means that this line and the next two must be kept together, so that the heading, if it is left at the end of a page, will have two lines under it. If this cannot be done, then the heading will appear on the next page.

If, on the other hand, you had some item that came at the end of a piece of text, and which you did not want to have placed on its own on a new page, you could type at the start of this line, [–]K3(ENTER), which would have the effect of keeping this line and the two lines above it together. These 'keep' commands are rather like hard spaces applied to page ends, and the number which is used determines how many lines are affected in this way. Both of these effects can be obtained from the **f6** menu, but this takes rather longer than the neat and simple way of typing the codes directly. You need to remember to press the ENTER key following the number part of each command, otherwise only the letter portion will appear, and the part of the SET or CLEAR menu which the command refers to will come up after a short delay, waiting for you to press ENTER.

In much document work these facilities are of little importance, because you can see where the breaks occur and shift text to suit. The exception is when you are changing type sizes and layouts, so that it becomes difficult to ensure that page breaks will be where you expect them. You may, for example, have a document on disc which was perfectly laid out, and then alter its layout and print without paying much attention to what is happening. The page break is a safety net against such carelessness, though it's really much more useful and necessary on the 'post-formatted' type of word processor.

Section Twelve
Printer Management

Paper

Most of the layouts included on the Start-of-day disc assume the use of the standard A4 and A5 sizes of paper which must be fed in one sheet at a time. This is the normal requirement for many word processing uses, and we should note at this point that the printer can handle paper which consists of one bond sheet and one or more bank flimsy copies, with thick skin carbons between. The dot matrix printer has sufficient impact on the paper to make reasonable carbon copies, though not with the clarity of a good electric typewriter or a daisywheel type of computer printer. One thing that has to be watched, however, is that some carbons, particularly the plastic type, allow paper to slip easily, so that the print rollers will slide one sheet in and leave the others. The old-fashioned 'paper' carbons give much less trouble.

For some purposes, however, you may want to work with paper in some continuous form. One such form is the teletype roll, which consists of plain paper 215 mm wide in rolls of about 3 inches in diameter. Your reason for using this might be that you want a draft copy produced quickly, with no need to attend to the printer. To use this paper, you will need to place the reel on a spindle, and put the spindle on a carrier of some sort. These items may be optional extras for the Amstrad printer, but I have not seen them advertised. If you enquire at computer shops, you should be able to find spindles and carriers for Seikosha printers which will be suitable. I pressed an Epson printer spindle and holder into service. You could just as easily knock up something suitable from an old Meccano outfit (though old Meccano sets are by now more valuable than computers!), or from light angle aluminium and rod, or even wood. This type of paper does not stay accurately in position, however, tending to slip to one side or the other. Unless guides are clipped to the printer to keep the paper from slipping sideways, the results are likely to be unsatisfactory.

Another way in which you are likely to find the use of continuous sheets unsatisfactory is the conflict of page layouts. If you try to reproduce a document of several pages with continuous paper, the most likely problem is that a page will be printed, then a blank page, then the next document page, and so on. This happens because the document will probably be set for 70 line pages, and continuous stationery usually assumes the use of 66 line pages. You can alter either the document header *or* the print size (using **f1** from the Printer menu) to make the two compatible, and in most cases it will be more convenient to set the Printer menu for 70 line working. The difficulty of keeping the paper in place remains, however, and the use of two-ply roll (two sheets separated by a one-shot carbon) is definitely not recommended, because the sheets nearly always separate.

On the whole, if you are going to use continuous stationery, the sprocketed type of paper is much more satisfactory. This also can be obtained in single, two, or three-ply form. Its use is certainly essential if you want to ensure that copy appears in exactly the correct place in each sheet, because the sprocket feed mechanism is much more positive than a roller, and will prevent any sideways movement of the paper. You will have to start by connecting the sprocket feed device which comes with your PCW 8256. This is a simple clip-in fit on the top of the printer. Raise the rear cover of the printer to a vertical position, and pull it up out of the way. Now hold the sprocket feed attachment so that the hollow portion which holds the sprockets and the roller is on top, and the small nylon gearwheel under the attachment is to your left. You will see that the sprocket drive attachment has four locating lugs on its lower corners, and these locate into four slots on top of the printer body. Engage the two front lugs of the sprocket feeder into the slots that are on each side of the printer roller, and then press in the back lugs. This clips the sprocket feed into place, and allows your printer to take sprocketed paper.

Now feed the paper into place. Put the printer offline (**f8**) and feed in a sheet using the roller and feeding by hand. Slide the two sprocket wheels sideways so that one is at the extreme left-hand side and the other is at the extreme right-hand side of the sprocket paper driver. You will find that each sprocket is covered by a hinged top casing, and these can be released by pulling them upwards on their inner edges, revealing the sprockets. Pull the paper central, and then slide in the sprocket wheels until the holes in the paper can be engaged with the sprockets. When the paper is central and the holes engaged in the sprockets on each side, clip down the covers over the sprocket wheels. If the paper looks rather crumpled, pull the sprockets *gently* apart until the paper straightens. You should find now that when you move the roller of the printer by hand, the sprockets will move too, keeping the paper precisely positioned. If the roller moves but the sprockets do not, then the most likely cause is that the sprocket drive attachment is not pushed fully down into place. Once this has been done, the drive should be completely positive, and there should be no buckling or puckering of the paper. You will have to arrange a shelf for the paper coming from the printer to rest on, otherwise there will be problems if the outcoming paper rests on the pile that is being fed into the printer.

This time, you will have to ensure compatability of paper and documents by altering the header for the documents. For the usual 11 inch fanfold paper that is supplied for these printers, the settings are shown on page 103 of the word processing manual. These settings ensure that each page will be printed correctly so that the pages will separate exactly at the perforations. This is critical, because if the settings are not correct there will inevitably be some text on the perforations between sheets after a few pages have been printed.

Correct paper settings are particularly important when the machine is being used for label printing. Self-adhesive labels can be bought attached to sprocketed paper, positioned so that a sheet of labels can be printed from a page of text. Here also, the layout of the text and the positioning of the paper is of vital importance. Only considerable practice will ensure that you get the text correctly positioned in each label. It is also important to set the top of form position for the first sheet in a set of continuous sheets. This is done by placing the paper so that the printhead is on the first line of the text. This might be a blank line, but for label printing it is more likely to be the first text line. The PTR key is then used to select the printer options, and key **f3** will allow you to take the 'Set top of form' option. Once this has been set for the first sheet, the printer should automatically set each new sheet to the same corresponding position, assuming that the number of lines and gap size are correctly set (66 lines and gap of 5 for 11 inch stationery). Figure 12.1 shows a layout onto fanfold paper for a set of labels. This is an imaginary pharmacist's label set for what I would take to be a regular customer. In most cases, labels of this type would carry a name and address, or would be made up of a set of customers' names and addresses, or a set of product names and descriptions and so on. Fanfold paper can be bought with a wide range of self-adhesive label sizes and types, and your local office suppliers will be pleased to show you the range.

The other options

There are several other printer options that we can explore at this stage. The only option on the printer **f1** menu that we have not looked at is the Paper out defeat. When this option is *not* ticked, the printer will stop whenever it is out of paper. This is therefore an option which we would take only when using continuous stationery. When the printer stops for this reason, there is no message on the screen, because the Main menu is normally being displayed rather than the Printer menu. Pressing the PRN key to bring up the Printer menu will also show the 'No paper' message next to the flashing 'Printer' legend at the top left-hand corner of the screen. The only reason for using the paper out signal with single sheet stationery is to safeguard against text which might overrun the paper. If, for example, you have a template for A5 paper and you want to see if a document on an A4 template will fit, it makes sense to remove the tick from the Paper out defeat so that if the text is likely to overrun, the printer will stop before it runs out of paper. When continuous stationery is being used, the Paperout defeat should be cancelled because we

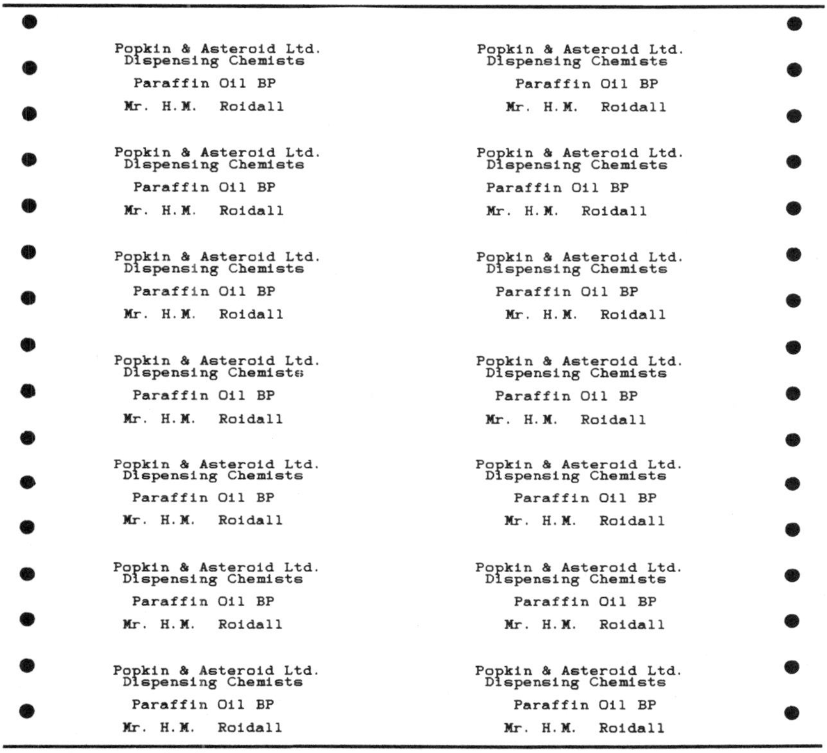

Figure 12.1. Using fanfold paper for label printing. Fanfold paper can be bought with a wide range of self-adhesive labels attached.

want the printer to stop if the paper runs out. This is particlarly important, because when continuous stationery is in use the printer is often left unattended as it chomps steadily through the sheets.

The **f2** menu for the printer brings up only one message, 'Clear Waiting for Paper'. This is for emergency use only, because normally the printer will restart when a new sheet of paper is put in. Even loading in paper without using the normal loading method will still cancel the Waiting for Paper warning. If the printer does appear to be waiting for no good reason, however, this option (press ENTER) will sort it out. In normal service it is never needed.

For many purposes, the **f3** Actions menu is useful and interesting. The items here are selected by moving the cursor and pressing the [+] key, and the menu stays on screen until the CAN or ENTER key is pressed. The top item of the menu is 'Feed one line', which allows you to press the [+] key and perform one paper line feed. This is particularly useful when you are using the machine with headed paper, and you want to position a sheet exactly. You have to use this with caution, however, because there is no provision for feeding in the reverse direction – pressing the [−] key produces only a beep. The action does not repeat if the [+] key is held down, so making it less easy to overrun. After each line feed, the current line number is shown on the top of the screen following the word 'Online'. When the paper is loaded, the words in this position are 'Top of form', and the next line, if you are using the default settings, will be Line 8, because the default setting is for a seven-line header. The next item down on this menu is 'Feed to top of form'. This makes the printer roll out the paper until it is almost clear of the rollers. If the paper has been loaded in the usual way, and has been advanced only by using the line feed option or by the normal action of printing lines, then the Top of form option will always allow the paper to be released, providing the paper is not larger than is catered for in the Form length option of the **f1** menu. For continuous stationery, the Top of form option allows you to run out exactly one page.

The third item down in this menu is 'Set top of form'. This is an option that you will normally want only when continuous stationery is being used. When you feed in the first edge of a continuous sheet, you can run it to the correct position for starting printing, and then set the Top of form option. This will ensure, providing the form length and gap have been correctly set, that the next page will start in exactly the same position. This is particularly important for such actions as label printing, or printing on headed sheets of continuous stationery. Note that where you set Top of form need not be the physical top of form. For example, if you wanted to print a couple of lines in the middle of each of two hundred sheets of continuous stationery forms, you could set the Top of form at the first line that would be printed, and make sure that your text ended with a form feed character. This done, you could start the printer, and each form would have its two lines printed, after which the printer would roll on to the centre of the next sheet. The Top of form option is not one that you would use with single sheets, because the act of loading a single sheet automatically sets the top of form.

The remaining option in this menu is the Offset size for left offset. The start of printing position that is assumed in template layouts is the extreme left-hand position of the printhead, and you would normally make use of the left margin to control where the head was moved to. If you need to position paper very much more accurately than can be done by guessing the centre position, then you may need offset. For example, if you guide the paper in along the right-hand edge of the printer, the starting position for the head will be too far to the left. The offset control allows this to be altered, moving the head to where the paper starts. Normally, you would use this only for direct printing, because using offset along with normal margins and shifted paper can result in losing words, usually from the end of a line. The offset is used by typing a number of spaces and pressing the [+] key. The offset can be continually altered in this way until it looks satisfactory, because the head is moved whenever the [+] key is pressed. When the offset position looks correct, the ENTER key can be used to remove the menu with the offset position maintained. An alternative method of specifying offset is to type in the number of offset spaces into the 'Offset size:' line.

The Document/Reprint menu

This Printer menu is obtained by using key **f5** after the PTR key has been pressed or paper loaded. If you are not actually printing a document at the time, the menu consists of one option only, Cancel. The menu becomes useful when you are printing a document, both for information and for repair. As an information source, it can be used when you load in the next sheet of paper to check the point you have reached in the printing. This is reported at the top of the sub-menu, with Filename, First page number, present (This) page number and Last page number listed. The other options can be used if anything goes wrong in printing and you have to repeat a section. I must emphasise that this is of limited use, because if you have noticed a misspelling in a page you cannot reprint the page with the spelling corrected, as you can with some other types of word processor. The main purpose of this menu exists to prevent a paper accident from spoiling a whole document. If, for example, you have carelessly loaded a sheet of paper or if the paper for some reason becomes mangled in the printer, this menu allows a limited scope for reprinting. The three options that appear are This page, Previous page and From beginning (and not as shown in the manual, page 117). The From beginning option is one that you would not normally use, because its just as easy to go back to the Main menu and use key **P** to start the printout from the beginning. The Previous page and This page options, however, are very useful once the paper has been sorted out. If you are using continuous stationery, you will have to remember to set the Top of form position again, because in the course of sorting out a tangle you will certainly have lost this position. The most common reason for paper problems with continuous stationery is letting the end of the printed paper get among the unprinted pile, so that it gets fed in again. You can avoid this by using a small shelf to hold the printed sheets, and computing magazines frequently contain advertisements for such items; they are also stocked by office suppliers. Single sheets usually give problems if the corners are slightly torn – they then load askew, but you should notice this at the time before you start printing. It's happily unusual for a correctly loaded sheet to start to give trouble, so this part of the Document/Reprint menu is one that is seldom needed.

The remaining keys which affect the printer are **f7** and **f8**. The f7 key is used to Abandon printing and reset the printer. This would normally be used only when a printout is obviously wrong (wrong file, for example) and you do not want printing to proceed to the bitter end. Using this option stops printing, sends the printhead to the left-hand side of the printer, and loses the Top of form position. After using this option, you cannot take up printing again on the same document except by restarting, using the **P** key. The **f8** key can be used to switch the printer on and off line. When you are printing a document, pressing the PTR key will halt and suspend printing, and pressing EXIT will restore printing. If, after pressing the PTR key you use **f8** to put the printer offline, you will not restart the printer when you press EXIT. This allows you to carry out some actions, such as copying a file or moving a file, but *not changing a disc*. To return to printing, you press the PTR key to get the Printer menu, and press f8 again to get online. Pressing EXIT now allows printing to take up where it left off. You can, of course, also carry out actions like replacing the paper or the ribbon while the printer is offline.

Section Thirteen
Disc Management

The Disc management menu is another name for the Main menu, in which all the group and filenames are displayed. When this menu is on screen, the title 'Disc management' appears on the top line, just to the left of centre. In this menu you can take the letter key options **C**, **E**, **P**, or **D** to create, edit or print a document, or go into direct printing mode. For some reason the **P** and **D** options are sometimes omitted from the display, but they still exist and will be obeyed when the Disc management menu is being displayed. When you use the **C** option, you will have the cursors placed over some group and filename, and the effect of **C** will be to bring up the appropriate template for that group. Failing a group template, the document creation will use the nearest available template, and if this is a new disc with no templates available, then the default manuscript template for A4 will be used. If you have put in an unformatted disc you will get an error report of 'Disc data error' when you try to use it, assuming you have not notified the disc change with **f1**. If you use **f1** on an unformatted disc you get the 'Disc format not recognised' message.

It is important to be clear about the use of templates in this respect. If you use the **C** key to create a new document, the template for this document will be the template that belongs to the group you have chosen. If you don't want to use this template but you *do* want to place a document in this group, you have two options. One is to copy a document from another group, and then edit it. This will retain its own template when it is recorded into the group that you have chosen. The other option is to keep a file of templates and to copy the one you want into the group you want to use, then use the **E** key to transform this into a document. Note in both cases the importance of copying. If you simply pick a document with some template and edit it, what you record on the disc is your new document, not the old template, unless you have worked on the TEMPLATE.STD file. This can make life confusing when you want to use the document template again. It's important to remember, particularly if you have been used to other word processing systems, that you cannot record under a changed filename. The filename that you use to record a document is the filename it had when you called it. Before we examine any of the other options in the Disc management menu, then, we shall look at the most important of the actions that we have not covered so far, recovering limbo files.

Limbo files

A limbo file results when a file has been edited. Unless the edit is abandoned without recording, the new and changed file will be recorded on to the disc *under the same filename*. Note, incidentally, that in LOCO SCRIPT there is no way of printing a file without recording it or having it already recorded on disc. This avoids the calamity of printing a document and switching off, then suddenly realising that you have thrown away all of the typing by not recording a file. When a file is recorded after editing, then, it will use the same filename as it had before, but the old version still exists. This old version is a 'limbo file', one whose name does not normally appear on the group listing. You can, however, discover how many limbo files exist by reading the message at the top of each group. This message reveals how many files have existed in previous versions, because there will be one limbo file for each file that has been edited.

To work with limbo files, you first of all need to list them, and this adds the limbo filenames to the group listing. You can then rename each limbo file that you want to resurrect, and the act of renaming will take the file out of limbo and into use. Only when a file is in use can it be edited or printed; these are actions that cannot be applied to limbo files. We shall look at each of these steps in order.

To find the names of limbo files, press key **f8** to bring up the Show options menu. This allows two choices, Limbo and Hidden. The hidden files are the files which are part of the LOCO SCRIPT system, and you don't normally need to know their names or sizes. The default is Limbo, and pressing the [+] key, then ENTER will reveal all of the limbo files, identified by the word 'limbo' following the name of the file. If you want to resurrect one limbo file, place the cursor over it.

To resurrect a selected limbo file, press the **f5** key, and move the cursor to 'recover from Limbo'. This will put a tick against this option, and you need only press ENTER. You will then see a sub-menu which reminds you of the name of the limbo file, and asks for a new name. You *must* use a name which is not already in use in that group. If you choose a name that already exists, you will get an error message to that effect, and the command will be abandoned. If you do not type a filename, but simply press ENTER, you will get the 'Invalid filename' message. You must type a suitable filename that is not already in use in that group and press ENTER. When you do so you will hear the disc spin, and the new name will be added as a valid file, in its correct position in alphabetical order in the list. This is now a file that you can edit and use once more.

To remove the limbo lists, press **f8** and take the tick off the Limbo option by pressing the [–] key. When you press ENTER, the listings will have the limbo filenames removed.

The other options

Disc management is so important that we shall now go through all the f-key options in the Disc management menu in detail. Unlike a typewriter, which has finished with a document as soon as the document leaves the type rollers, a word processor depends very heavily on the use of discs. This is particularly true of LOCO SCRIPT, because of the way that the disc action is bound up with editing and printing. Another factor to consider is the use of the M drive, consisting of memory only but arranged to use the same commands as a disc drive. The use of the M drive can overcome some of the problems that you might encounter if you have only a single disc drive on your PCW 8256.

Disc changing

When you remove one disc and insert another, you must press the **f1** key so that the new Disc management menu can be read from the new disc and displayed. If you do not do this you will encounter serious problems. It will not, for example, be possible to save your edited text if you have changed a disc without notification – you cannot do this even if you *do* attempt to notify a disc change. The most important point is that you need to notify the disc change in order to make the Disc management menu correspond with what is on the disc. Failure to do this means that you could ask to edit a file that appears on the screen but is not on the current disc. An attempt to do this will bring up the message 'Disc has been changed' as a reminder. You need to press ENTER to remove the message and notify the change (so that **f1** will not be needed).

To save a file on another disc you need to make use of the M drive. The technique is to copy the file to the M drive, change discs, notify using **f1**, and then copy from the M drive into Drive A (assuming one disc drive only). For copying techniques, see later in this section. Remember that if you have edited a file in Drive A and the result of editing makes the file too long to fit back, you cannot put the file into the M drive to transfer subsequently to another disc. As it happens, the disc will be used intermittently as you add text to a file, and when the disc fills, you will be informed that there is no more space. You can then transfer the existing file to the M drive, hence to another disc, and from there carry on editing.

Inspect and Copy

The **f2** key is labelled 'Inspect', and its purpose is to allow you to preview the contents of a document. This is possible only if an Identify summary has been typed in a previous edit (see Section 7; the Identify action has been dealt with in that section). Of more interest now is the **f3** key, which produces the Copy action.

To copy a file you must first have the cursor over the file that you need to copy. Having done this, press the f3 key. You will see a brief message at the top of the screen to the effect that you should place the group cursor over the destination drive and group. The file cursor will also move, but this is not important – don't worry if the filename cursor happens to be over a file. When you press ENTER, you will see the file transferred and, as usual, the file will be inserted in the group listing in the correct alphabetical position. This concludes the Copy action.

The Copy can be to any group and any drive that is connected. For a single drive machine, you have the options of Drive A or Drive M. A Copy to Drive M puts the file into memory so that the disc can be changed and a new disc inserted (remember to press f1). The file can then be copied from the M drive group into a group on the new disc, using the same copying technique as described above. Note that the Copy action leaves the original file unchanged, so that after a Copy action you have an extra copy of the file, not just a shifted file. The alternative to this is to Move the file.

To move a file, you start by placing the cursor of the Disc manager on the filename that you want to move. Now press key f4, which will bring up the request to move the cursor to the destination drive and group. When you have done this, pressing ENTER will carry out the move, *and delete the old file*. Because the old file is deleted, you need to carry out this action with much more care than a Copy. Unless you are very certain, in fact, you should use Copy and Erase rather than Move when you want to shift files. Remember, in particular, that if you move a file from disc to the M drive, the file will exist only in memory from that point on, and any interruption of power will cause the whole file to be lost. If you had used Copy, the original would have remained on the disc.

The next option of the Disc management menu is renaming, and this allows several varieties of renaming to be carried out. You can rename a disc, rename a group, rename a file or recover a document from limbo. We have dealt with the limbo option already, and we shall concentrate now on the other options.

To rename a document, place the cursor over this option (the default) and press ENTER. You will see a reminder of the present document name, and you can now type the new name in its place. As usual, the name can consist of up to eight characters of main name, then a dot and up to three characters of extension. The usual editing actions of the DEL keys apply, and when you have finished typing the new name, the action is confirmed by pressing ENTER.

To erase a file, place the file cursor over the filename and press the f6 key. This will bring up a reminder, and the file is erased when the ENTER key is used to confirm. You cannot erase a filename if it also happens to be the file you are working on. This is important, because you may have to erase files in order to make room on a disc, and this may have to be done while editing is in progress (see Disc management while editing, later this section). If in doubt, erase all limbo files.

The remaining two sets of f-key actions are a mixed bag. The menu that you get by using f7 is simply the Edit, Print, Create, Direct set of actions that you can summon up in any case by typing the first letters of each. The only advantage of using these commands from this menu is that you have the chance to cancel with the CAN key if you change your mind in time. The f8 menu is the one that allows limbo and hidden files to be displayed. If you examine the hidden files, you will find that there is a file called MAIL232 in Group 0. This is not a LOCO SCRIPT file, but one that runs under the CP/M operating system to provide an electronic mail system if you have suitable hardware.

Disc management during editing

Disc management during editing is one of the most difficult arts to master in the operation of your PCW 8256. To show how the principle is used, I shall describe here how a file can be created and filled with text from another non-LOCO SCRIPT source, in this case a file of instructions from a CP/M disc. If you have not used CP/M at all and feel that you are missing something, then I recommend that you read the description in my book, *Advanced Amstrad CPC6128 Computing*, published by Collins. I have another book, for devotees only, called *Introducing Amstrad CP/M Assembly Language*, also published by Collins. The point is that other uses of the computer can produce other files on other discs. Not all of these files can be read into LOCO SCRIPT form, only the files which are of the type called ASCII. Files which are not ASCII will produce at best only a few odd-looking character shapes; at worst they will cause effects like clearing the screen, sounding the beeper, or making the disc drive operate for no obvious reason. This illustration concerns reading a file called ESCHAR.ASM from a CP/M disc, starting with a data disc and LOCO SCRIPT. If you have no such files to read, then this part of this section can be skipped.

Start by choosing a suitable group and template. I picked the manuscript group, and then copied this into a group in Drive M. Keeping the cursor on this group, I then used key C to request a new document. The name chosen was ASM.001, and this was typed into the space that appeared for the title. Pressing ENTER then confirmed this name, and set up the file ready for use. The screen then displayed the normal editing menu. Pressing f7 then brought up the Editing sub-modes menu. The last item of this set is Disc management, and the cursor was moved to this legend, and ENTER pressed. This gave the Disc management menu, with the reminder on the top of the screen that this is 'Disc management whilst editing'. The text disc was then removed, and the CP/M disc containing the file ESCHAR.ASM was put in, and key f1 was pressed to notify disc change. Note that *you cannot carry out a disc change of this type if you are using a file from the disc*. This action was possible only because the file was taken from Drive M. As far as the computer is concerned, what goes on in Drive A is irrelevant to Drive M and is permitted. The reminder phrase, 'Using M' appears at the top right-hand side of the screen throughout this time. Pressing EXIT then put the text template back on the screen, and f7 was pressed again, this time to select Insert text. Pressing ENTER on this produced the listing of files for the CP/M disc, and file ESCHAR was selected in the usual way. Most CP/M discs will produce listings that consist entirely of Group 0 files. This is because the files in a LOCO SCRIPT listing are grouped in a way that corresponds to USER numbers in CP/M. Most CP/M files are for USER 0 (the default) and unless your CP/M disc is used by several people, all its files will be in Group 0. Pressing ENTER copied the text into the LOCO SCRIPT file, and pressing EXIT allowed the file to be recorded, without printing. This was still in Drive M, and with the Disc management menu on the screen the disc was changed again, back to the LOCO SCRIPT data disc. The file in Drive M was then copied into a group in Drive A, completing the transfer.

It's not so complicated as it sounds when you read it over, and the underlying principles are important. If you are likely, in the course of working on a document, to need to use several discs, then a copy of the document should be put into Drive M, or the document created using a Drive M group and template. This will allow discs to be changed at will, and material copied from disc to Drive M or vice versa as much as you like. This gets around the problem that we have encountered, that a disc cannot be changed while a file on that disc is being edited – this is because a file always exists partly on the disc and partly in the memory. By specifying Drive M, we eliminate this problem. The penalty we pay for this freedom is that an interruption of power will kill the file, so any file that is being edited in Drive M should be copied to a disc at intervals.

Section Fourteen
The Menu HELP Pages

The following pages are arranged to provide quick help in getting around the various menus of the PCW 8256. Each page describes a set of actions and the key sequence that is needed to carry out the actions. Because different menus are available from different states (printer just loaded, editing being done, disc management etc.), the starting condition is given first, then the key sequence and the method of choosing. Where the choices are taken from a sub-menu, the appropriate choice is shown in italics, and the default type is in bold. The key sequence for choice is then shown. For clarity, only the section of menu that is relevant to the subject is shown.

HELP List

Character style
Copy document
Disc change
Disc management
Edit base layout
Edit header/footer
Emphasised printing
Erase document
Header/footer text
Identify document
Insert text from disc
Inspect blocks/phrases
Layout and Tab count
Layout change in document
Line layout
Modes of action
Move document
Page breaks
Page layout
Page numbers
Page size
Paper feed
Paper size, layout
Paper size, printer
Paper type
Print quality
Printer switching
Printhead movement
Printing status
Renaming actions
Reprint
Reset printer
Reveal filenames
Save blocks/phrases
Show markers
Zero and decimal

Character style

Choices: Half height, italic, pitch on line.

Starting point: Create/Edit menu (press **C** or **E** from Disc management menu).

Press **f4**.

Character style

  – **Half Height**
  – Italic
  – Pitch ??

Choose by moving cursor and using [+] or [–] keys.

Sub-menus:

Half Height –

    SupeRscript
    SuBscript

Choose with cursor and [+] or [–] keys.

Pitch –

    10 pitch
    12 pitch
    15 pitch
    17 pitch
    Prop. spacing

    normal width
    Double width

Choose with cursor and [+] or [–] keys.

Press ENTER to confirm choices, CAN to cancel.

Quick alternative: Press [+] key, followed by letter(s) in caps from list above. Where number is needed following capital letter, type number and press ENTER. For example, [+]P12D(ENTER) selects 12-pitch, double width. Also obtainable from SET menu (press[+] and chequer keys).

Copy document

Choices: Source, destination, confirm/cancel.

Starting point: Disc management menu.

Choose source document by moving cursor.

Press f3.

Title and reminder on top screen.

Choose destination group with cursor.

Press ENTER to copy, CAN to cancel action.

Note: Copy action does not delete source file.

Disc change

Change disc or disc side.

Starting point: Disc management menu (Main menu). During editing, this can be reached by using the Modes (**f7**) menu.

Press **f1** after changing disc.

Note: This must not be attempted if a document is being edited from the same drive. Copy document to Drive M and edit/create from this drive if disc changing is needed. See Section 13 for details.

Disc management

Choice: Transfer temporarily to Disc management menu from Editing menu.

Starting point: Create/Edit menu (press **C** or **E** from Disc management menu).

Press **f7**.

Move cursor to Disc management menu.

Press ENTER.

Return by pressing EXIT.

Note: Not all options of disc management are open. You cannot change discs if you are editing a document in the current disc drive, and you cannot print a document while it is being edited from that drive. These restrictions can be overcome by using Drive M as the document source/destination for editing.

Edit base layout

Choices: Complete base layout, including line pitch, character pitch, style, pagination, header and footer text.

Starting point: Create/Edit menu (press **C** or **E** from Disc management menu).

Press **f7**.

Choose **Edit header** (default) with cursor, press ENTER.

Header/footer text appears. This text can be edited now or later after editing remainder of base layout.

To proceed, press **f7**.

This brings up Editing header screen. This can be used now or later.

To edit layout, press **f1**.

> Choices: character pitch, line pitch, line space, italic, justify. Choices of pitch and space made by moving cursor across and typing number. Numbers must be in permitted ranges. Italic and justify selected by using [+] key. Justify means **fully justify**, both left and right.
>
> Move cursor down to first line of text, and use f-keys.
>
> Position cursor at desired left margin position, press **f1**.
>
> Position cursor at desired right-hand margin, press **f2**.
>
> Position cursor at desired TAB position(s), press **f3**, **f4**, **f5**, **f6** according to tab required.
>
> Delete existing TABs by placing cursor over tab and pressing [-] key.
>
> Press EXIT to return to Editing header menu.

For other details see entries for:
Character style, Layout and Tab count, Page breaks, Page layout, Page numbers, Header/footer text.

Note: Layout editing menu above can also be obtained from **f2** key choice in Editing menu, but this applies to numbered layout change in document only, not to base layout.

Edit header/footer

Choice: Text for headers and footers.

Starting point: Create/Edit menu (press **C** or **E** from Disc management menu).

Press **f7**.

Place cursor on **Edit header** (default), press ENTER.

This brings up header and footer text on normal text editing screen.

After editing, press EXIT.

Exit pagination editing

Use this pagination
Recover old pagination
Empty pagination text
Abandon edit altogether

Choose with cursor, press ENTER to confirm.

Note: Empty option is useful to delete old headers and footers quickly.

Emphasised printing

Choices: Underline, bold, double strike, reverse video. Only underline and reverse video appear on screen. Reverse video does not print on paper.

Starting point: Create/Edit menu (press **C** or **E** from Disc management menu).

Press **f3**.

Emphasis codes

- **Underline**

- Bold
- Double
- ReVerse Video

Choose by moving cursor and pressing [+] or [-] keys. Confirm choices by pressing ENTER.

Quick alternative: Press [+] key, followed by letters shown in caps above (such as **U**, **B**, **D**, **RVV**).

Note: Underlining and reverse video show on screen. Double and bold do not appear, but does will be shown if selected in the **f1** menu. Reverse video does not print; it is used to mark text for attention on screen, such as text to be deleted.

Erase document

Choices: File to be erased, confirm or cancel.

Starting point: Disc management menu.

Press **f6**.

Erase document
___

Name: NAMEDOC.001
Group: O
Drive: A

Choose to erase document indicated by cursor, name group and drive
as indicated *or* type in new name, group, drive as needed.

Press ENTER to confirm, CAN to cancel.

Note: A limbo file can be erased completely in this way, provided its
name is on display, with the cursor placed over it. You cannot delete
a limbo file simply by typing its name. See Renaming actions.

Header/footer text

Choice: Text to appear in headers and footers, including page numbers.

Starting point: Editing header page (see Base layout menu), then pressing EXIT *or* by pressing **f7** from text editing.

Top of screen shows title 'Editing pagination'.

Cursor is placed in position for Header 1. Type text for this header and press RETURN. Move cursor to start of Footer 1, type text, press RETURN. Repeat for as many headers and footers as will be used. Reminder text underneath (not printed on paper) shows how headers and footers will be used. The normal centring, bold, underlining etc. effects can be used.

Page numbering:
 The page numbers have to be inserted using the **f6** menu, or by typing [+]PN for page number or [+]LPN for last page number. This code must be followed by the position indicators =, <, or > to indicate centred, left or right. The maximum number of digits in the page number must be allowed for by using the correct number of signs, usually three.

When header/footer text and number are complete, press EXIT.

Exit pagination editing:

Use this pagination
Recover old pagination
Empty pagination text
Abandon edit altogether

Choose with cursor, press ENTER to confirm, CAN to cancel.

Identify document

Choices: Create or inspect summary of document.

Creation

Starting point: Text editing menu called by using **C** or **E** from Disc management menu.

Press **f7**.

Editor sub-modes:

> **Edit header**
> *Edit Identify text*
> Insert text
> Disc management

Choose with cursor, confirm with ENTER.

(Space for three lines
of text, total 30
characters)

Type text (DEL keys and cursor shift keys can be used). Press ENTER when finished. Text is recorded along with document. If edit of document is abandoned, this text will also be lost.

Inspection

Starting point: Disc management menu.

Press **f2**.

Name: DOCNAME
Group: 0
Drive: A

Three line summary
of document appears
here.

Remove with CAN or ENTER.

Insert text from disc

Choice: Text can be any LOCO SCRIPT text, or ASCII coded file from CP/M. Will be inserted in current document.

Starting point: Create/Edit menu (press **C** or **E** from Disc management menu).

Press **f7**.

Edit header
Edit Identify text
Insert text
Disc management

Choose by moving cursor to Insert text, then press ENTER.

Disc management menu is then displayed. Use cursor to pick *source group and filename*. Press ENTER to confirm, CAN to cancel.

Note: Top of screen message refers incorrectly to *destination* Group and drive.

Inspect blocks/phrases

Choices: Inspect block numbers and phrase letters allocated.

Starting point: Create/Edit menu (press **C** or **E** from Disc management menu).

Press **f8**.

Sub-menu shows block numbers of blocks used, and letters allocated to phrases.

Layout and Tab count

Choice: Up to 99 layouts in a document, up to 99 tab position in each layout.

Starting point: Editing header page (see Base layout) menu.

Press **f5**.

Maximums:

25 layouts
16 tabs each

Choose by moving cursor, typing in number.

Confirm arrangement by pressing ENTER.

Returns to Edit header menu.

Note: Space is reserved on disc for the number of layouts/tabs selected. To conserve disc space, allow only as many as are likely to be needed. Using cursor right or left keys when typing the number gives digits 3 and 1 respectively.

Layout change in document

Choices: Start brand new layout, use established layout number, revert to base layout, edit layout (not base layout).

Starting point: Create/Edit menu (press **C** or **E** from Disc management menu).

Press **f2**.

Document layout
    Insert layout

---

    brand New layout
    Layout   ??
    Base layout

    Edit layout
    Layout   ??

Choose by cursor, type layout number if needed as indicated by question marks.

Press ENTER to confirm choice, CAN to cancel.

Quick alternative: For change of numbered layout, press [+]LTn(ENTER), where 'n' indicates number. Else use SET menu by pressing [+] and chequer key.

Note: The base layout cannot be altered by this menu, which is concerned only with changes of layout within the document. You can, however, start with a brand new layout and use this for the whole document if the base layout is not suitable.

Line layout

Choose: Centre line, right justify (not left), soft or hard space or hyphen, line spacing and pitch.

Staring point: Create/Edit menu (press **C** or **E** from Disc management menu).

Press **f5**.

Line layout:

Centre line
Right Justify line

---

insert soft space
insert hard space
insert soft hyphen
insert hard hyphen

Line Spacing   ??
Line Pitch   ?

Select with cursor, [+] or [-] key, type number where ? appears.

Line Spacing choice is 0, 1, $1\frac{1}{2}$, 2, $2\frac{1}{2}$, 3.
Line Pitch choice is **6 lines per inch** (default) or 8 lines per inch. This sets the size of single line spacing.

Choice is made when [+] key is pressed, or number is typed followed by ENTER.

Quick Alternative: Press [+] key followed by codes **C**, **RJ**, spacebar or hyphen, **LSn**(ENTER), **LPn**(ENTER). Also [-] key with space or hyphen for soft versions. Also obtainable from SET/CLEAR menus.

Note: The effect is noted on text screen if Codes choice has been made in **f1** menu.

Modes of action

Choices: Create, edit, print or direct printing.

Starting point: Disc management menu.

Either:
Press key **C**, **E**, **P** or **D** for action.
or
Press **f7**.
Select by cursor.
Confirm with ENTER or cancel with CAN.

Note: Normally simpler to use letter keys, but using **f7** allows cancellation before pressing ENTER. Note that if the **f7** menu is obtained when the Disc management menu has been called from the Edit menu, then only the Print option is shown. This, however, *cannot be used* on a document that is being edited.

Move document

Choices: Source document, destination group, confirm or cancel.

Starting point: Disc management menu.

Place cursor on chosen source document.

Press **f4**.

Title and reminder at top of screen.

Place cursor over destination group.

Press ENTER to move file, CAN to cancel action.

Note: Moving a file deletes the original version. Preferable not to move a file into Drive M; use Copy instead.

Page breaks

Choices: Widows & orphans prevented or allowed, broken paragraphs prevented or allowed.

Starting point: Editing header page (see Base layout menu).

Press **f6**.

Page breaks:

Widows & orphans

> **Prevented**
> Allowed

Broken paragraphs

> Prevented
> **Allowed**

Choose by moving cursor and pressing [+] or [-] keys. Default is widows and orphans prevented, broken paragraphs allowed.

Confirm choices by pressing ENTER.

Returns to Edit header menu.

Page layout

Choices: End of page position in text, page number in header.

Starting point: Create/Edit menu (press **C** or **E** from Disc management menu).

Press **f6**.

Page layout

---

end page here
Last Line of page

Keep lines together
   Above ??
   Below ??

---

insert page number
this Page Number
Last Page Number

Choose by moving cursor and pressing [+]. If number has to be typed, type it and press ENTER.

Quick alternative: For last line, press ALT RETURN. Use [+] key, then codes **LL**, **Kn**(ENTER), **PN**, **LPN**. To keep lines below, use [–]**Kn**(ENTER).

Note: Difference between end page here (at cursor position) or Last Line of page (i.e. new page after end of this line – but code need not be at end of line.

Page numbers

Choices: Starting number for pages, differences between pages in respect of header/footer text or presence/absence.

Starting point: Editing header page (see Base layout menu).

Press **f8**.

Pagination:

First page number   1

All pages same
First page differs
Last page differs
Odd/even pages differ

First page
   Header enabled
   Footer enabled

Last page
   Header enabled
   Footer enabled

Choose by moving cursor and pressing [+] or [-] keys except for page number choice, which needs number typed only if first page is not numbered 1.

Confirm choices by pressing ENTER, cancel with CAN.

Note: Combination of choices here of header and footer enabling work along with header/footer text editing. If no header or footer is wanted, then this section can be ignored. Providing no header or footer text is typed, nothing will appear.

Page size

Choices: Page length, header and footer sizes, header and footer positions. All measured in standard $\frac{1}{6}$ inch lines.

Starting point: Editing header page (see Base layout menu).

Press **f7**.

Page size:	
Page length	**70**
Header zone	9
position	6
page body	54
Footer zone	7
position	66

Select by moving cursor and typing new numbers if needed. Deleting a choice returns default, which is for A4.

Confirm by pressing ENTER, cancel with CAN.

Note: Impossible choices are signalled. Using cursor right and left keys gives number 3 and 1 respectively.

Paper feed

Choice: Feed one line, form feed, set top of form.

Starting point: Printer menu (load paper or press **PTR** key).

Press **f3**.

+ to:

Feed one line
Feed to top of form
Set top of form

Choose with [+] key.

Menu remains until CAN or ENTER pressed.

Paper size, layout

Choices: Overall length, size of header and footer zones, position of header and footer text.

Unit of size: Standard line width of $\frac{1}{6}$ inch or $\frac{1}{8}$ as set by base layout.

Starting point: Create or Edit menu.

Press **f7** Modes menu.
Edit header (default cursor position.) Press ENTER.
Press **f7** Options menu.
Press **f7** Page size menu.

Page size:	
Page length	**70**
Header zone	9
position	6
page body	54
Footer zone	7
position	66

Default settings: Depend on template used. Ultimate default is A4.

Choose by moving cursor and typing new numbers. The numbers represents units of $\frac{1}{6}$ inch (or $\frac{1}{8}$ inch) measured from the top of the page. The footer position should be a number less than the page length figure and more than the page body + footer zone figure.

Important note: An error message will be delivered if a combination of figures is impossible. The layout in this header must match the paper layout for the printer, particularly if continuous stationery is to be used.

Paper size, printer

Choices: Number of lines, number of gaps.
Unit of size: Standard line of $\frac{1}{6}$ inch or $\frac{1}{8}$ inch as set in base layout.

Starting point: Printer menu (load paper or press PTR key).

Press **f1**.

Form length:	**70**
Gap length:	**3**
Paper out defeat	

Default settings:
    For A4 paper when single sheet used.
    For 11 inch continuous when this selection made.

Choose by placing cursor and typing new figures if needed. Default values will return if DEL key is used.

Important note: The form length and gap size figures must tally with the layout values.

Paper type

Choices: Single sheet or continuous.

Starting point: Printer menu (load paper or press PTR key).

Press **f1**.

Single sheet paper
Continuous stationery

Choose with cursor and [+] or [−] key.
(Either/or choice)

Press ENTER to fix.

Print quality

Choices: Draft quality or high quality.
Starting point: Printer menu (load paper or press PTR key).

Press **f1**.

High quality
Draft quality

Choose with cursor and [+] or [-] key.
(Either/or choice)

Press ENTER to fix choice.

Printer switching

Choices: Online or offline.

Starting point: Printer menu (load paper or press PTR key).

Press **f8** (no menu appears).

Printer status report will change between online and offline each time this key is pressed.

Printhead movement

Choice: Position of printhead from left-hand side, in $\frac{1}{10}$ inch units.

Starting point: Printer menu (load paper or press PTR key).

Press f3.

Set left offset
Offset size: **0**

Choose with cursor and typing number.

Note: Useful mainly for direct printing because there is no layout to set left margin.

Printing status

Report: On filename, first, last and current page numbers.

Starting point: Printer menu obtained by pressing PTR key *during printout*.

Press **f5**.

File: Filename.ext
    First page   nnn
    This page   nnn
    Last page   nnn

Report only, no choice needed.

Press ENTER or CAN to remove report.

Renaming actions

Choices: Rename document, group, disco or limbo file.
Starting point: Disc management menu.

Press **f5**.

---

rename document
recover from Limbo
rename Group
rename Disc

Choose with cursor, confirm with ENTER

Note: Renaming a limbo file will make this into an active file. No file can be renamed with the name of an active file in the same group.

Reprint

Choices: Reprint present page, previous page, or complete document.

Starting point: Printer menu, obtained by pressing PRT key during a printout.

Press **f5**.

Reprint

This page
Previous page
From beginning

Choose with cursor and ENTER key.

Message appears: Reposition paper at top of form before allowing printing to continue.

Actions: Use can key, then **f3** to set Top of form. Back to **f5**, select page to reprint, press ENTER, then EXIT.

Reset printer

Choices: Reset or cancel.

Starting point: Printer menu (load paper or press PTR key).

Press **f7**.

Abandon printing and reset
   Confirm
   Cancel

Choose with cursor, confirm with ENTER.

Note: All settings of page number etc. are lost.

Reveal filenames

Choose: To reveal limbo or hidden files.

Starting point: Disc management menu.

Press **f8**.

Show options

Limbo
Hidden

Choose with cursor *and* [+] or [–] keys.

Press ENTER to confirm, CAN to cancel.

Note: Makes limbo files available for renaming or deleting. Hidden files are word processing and CP/M programs on LOCO SCRIPT disc.

Save blocks/phrases

Choices: Save numbered block or save all phrases.

Starting point: Create/Edit menu (press **C** or **E** from Disc management menu).

Press **f8**.

Text storage

Block

Save block   ??

Phrase (list)

Save all phrases

To save block move cursor to Save block option, type number of block. Press ENTER.

Disc management menu appears – top line message to pick destination drive and group. Do this by moving cursor, then press ENTER.

Save block

Name ?
Group XXXXXX
Drive A

Type name for block, confirm group and drive or alter. Press ENTER to confirm and execute.

Returns to Edit/Create screen.

Save all phrases:

Move cursor to this line, press [+] or ENTER to save phrases as PHRASES.STD file.

Show markers

Choices: Codes, rulers, blanks, spaces, effectors.

Starting point: Create/Edit menu (press **C** or **E** from Disc management menu).
Press **f1**.

Show state of

Codes
Rulers
Blanks
Spaces
Effectors

Choose with cursor and [+] or [-] keys. Choices confirmed with ENTER, cancelled with CAN.

Note: These choices can be switched on and off as desired at any stage in editing.

Zero and decimal

Choices: Zero slashed or unslashed, decimal point or comma.

Starting point: Editing header page (see Base layout menu).

Press **f3**

Characters:

Zero is Ø
Zero is 0

Decimal is .
Decimal is ,

Choose by moving cursor, pressing [+] or [–] keys.

Confirm choice with ENTER, cancel with CAN.

Returns to Edit header menu.

Appendix A
The ALT Character Set

⅛	ALT 1		¼	ALT 2
⅜	ALT 3		½	ALT 4
⅝	ALT 5		¾	ALT 6
⅞	ALT 7			
⅞	ALT 8		Å	ALT SHIFT 8
æ	ALT 9		Æ	ALT SHIFT 9
ø	ALT 0		Ø	ALT SHIFT 0
±	ALT -			
≃	ALT =		≡	ALT SHIFT =
∂	ALT q		∈	ALT e
ρ	ALT r		τ	ALT t
ψ	ALT y		↑	ALT u
⊗	ALT i		⊙	ALT SHIFT i
ω	ALT o		Ω	ALT SHIFT o
π	ALT p		Π	ALT SHIFT P
α	ALT a		Σ	ALT SHIFT s
σ	ALT s		Δ	ALT SHIFT d
δ	ALT d		∅	ALT f
γ	ALT g		Γ	ALT SHIFT g
←	ALT h		↔	ALT j
→	ALT k		λ	ALT l
∴	ALT ;		⇐	ALT SHIFT s
≤	ALT s		⇒	ALT SHIFT #

⩾	ALT #		x	ALT x
ß	ALT b		↓	ALT n
µ	ALT m		ç	ALT SHIFT ,
ç	ALT ,		∘	ALT SHIFT .
∘	ALT .		×	ALT SHIFT /
÷	ALT /		∞	ALT ½

Number lock ALT relay Caps lock   ALT ENTER

Appendix B
The EXTRA Character Set

¡	EXTRA 1	¨	EXTRA 2
℞	EXTRA 3	¢	EXTRA 4
˙	EXTRA 5	´	EXTRA 6
^	EXTRA 7	`	EXTRA 8
↔	EXTRA 9	Ø	EXTRA 0
~	EXTRA -	≠	EXTRA =
®	EXTRA r	™	EXTRA t
¥	EXTRA y	↑	EXTRA u
º	EXTRA o	¶	EXTRA p
ª	EXTRA a	ß	EXTRA s
†	EXTRA d	ƒ	EXTRA f
↑	EXTRA ;	«	EXTRA g
»	EXTRA #	©	EXTRA c
ß	EXTRA b	¦	EXTRA .
¿	EXTRA /	\	EXTRA ½

Number key pad on right does *not* give digits with EXTRA.
To use number pad, press ALT RELAY together, same to clear.
Note: ¥ on screen appears as ♀ .

Appendix C
Typing Accented Letters

1. Select accented or special letter from keyboard, using ALT or EXTRA as needed. Examples ç or ø.

2. Type accent first, then letter. Most of the accent marks are in the EXTRA set, notably EXTRA 6 and EXTRA 8. *Example*: EXTRA 6 and e gives é, EXTRA 8 and a gives à.

3. If you need the accent mark *without* the letter, type the accent and then press ENTER. Examples ´ ` ° ^ ¨.

Appendix D
Some Useful Addresses

Millway Stationery Ltd.
Chapel Hill
Stansted
Essex CM24 8AP
Tel: (0279) 8712009 (office hours)

Suppliers of general stationery, including A4 and A5 in reams at very low prices. Also stock a good range of continuous stationery for computer use.

Pinner Wordpro
34 Cannonbury Avenue
Pinner
Middx. HA5 1TS
Tel: (01) 868 9548 (any time)

Suppliers of printer ribbons, paper, labels, printer covers and accessories. Supply discs at very competitive prices, now including Amstrad discs.

Willis Computer Supplies Ltd.
PO Box 10
South Mill Road
Bishop's Stortford
Herts. CM23 3DN
Tel: (0279) 506491 (office hours)

Lowest prices for teletype rolls and some other items of continuous stationery. Excellent catalogue, with much of interest to the computer user.

Inmac (UK) Ltd.
Davy Road
Astmoor
Runcorn
Cheshire WA7 1PZ
Tel: 09285 67551 (Runcorn 24-hour service)
(Branch offices in London and other cities)

Suppliers mainly to large-scale users, with large delivery charge, but some very competitive prices. Good catalogue, delivered monthly. Excellent for priority delivery, by helicopter if you can afford it!

New Star Software Ltd.
45 Plovers Mead
Doddinghurst
Brentwood
Essex CM15 0PS
Tel: (0277) 823747 (office hours)

Suppliers of software of all kinds for all Amstrad machines. Of particular interest is NewWord, an alternative to LOCO SCRIPT for word processing. Office standards such as Supercalc-II, DBase-II are also available.

Mine of Information Ltd.
1 Francis Avenue
St. Albans
Herts. AL3 6BL
Tel: (0727) 52801

Almost certainly the best-stocked sellers of computer books in the UK. Their list is always worth looking at if you are looking for a book on any aspect of computing, professional or amateur, at any level of difficulty.

IDS Computer Supplies
15 Darin Court
Crownhill
Milton Keynes MK8 0AD
Tel: (0908) 569655

One of the few suppliers of discs stocking the 3 inch disc size. Prices are good on a box of 10 discs, and include delivery but not VAT.

Index

NORMAL CREEN WIDTH 90 CHARACTERS IN 12 PITCH